Clergy Stress: Causes and Cures clergy and Christian leaders Westafer's wisdom and practical every chapter. His use of humor sprinkled ... keeps the reader engaged as this difficult subject of stress is presented. If clergy will follow his advice, a more abundant life in ministry can be achieved as they serve. The timing of this book for this generation is critical.

-- Mark and Sheila Bagwell,
Shade Tree Ministries, Seneca, SC

Clergy Stress: Causes and Cures is a valuable resource for ministers whether they have experienced conflict, forced termination, or consider themselves to be healthy. It offers great examples of what happens within churches when conflict arises, which often is caused by change. Dr. Westafer is on target with ways for ministers to care for themselves, in addition to suggesting outside resources to help them reclaim their ministries.

-- Catherine Ralcewicz, Executive Director,
Ministering to Ministers Foundation, Inc.
Richmond, VA

Bill Westafer writes from a wealth of practical experience in handling the unique stress challenges of pastoral ministry. In his book, *Clergy Stress: Causes and Cures*, his personal antidotes, coupled with practical means to deal with stress, allows for a pastor to have handles to grab hold. All pastors experience stress. Once you recognize this and are ready to deal with stress effectively, this book will be a fantastic resource.

-- Dr. Phil Stevenson, District Superintendent,
Pacific Southwest District, The Wesleyan Church

Clergy Stress

Causes and Cures

Bill Westafer, Ed.D.

Kindle Direct Publishing
Independent Publishing/AMAZON

ISBN: 9781697236163

Clergy Stress: Causes and Cures
Author: Bill Westafer, Ed.D.

Dedication
To my wonderful children, Sara and Aaron.
"We went through fire and water, but God brought
us to a place of abundance"
(Psalm 66:12).
I love you.

TABLE OF CONTENTS

Acknowledgments

I wish to thank Dr. Edna Ellison for believing in this project and making it a reality. I am also grateful to Vickie Holt for her publishing expertise and cover design.

This book would not have been possible without the cooperation of the pastors interviewed for the study. I am thankful for their vulnerability and transparency. Their names were changed to provide anonymity.

Thank you to my sister, Cynthia Davis. She helped edit some of the chapters. She is a gifted grammarian and confidante.

Dr. Bob and Cheryl Moeller, *For Better For Worse For Keeps Ministries* co-founders, encouraged me with their prayers, counsel, and advice. I am grateful for all you've done for me personally and professionally.

Thank you to Dr. Charles Chandler and the *Ministering to Ministers Foundation* for inviting me to one of their Wellness Retreats when I experienced a dark time in my life.

My ministry knowledge evolved as a result of the pastors who risked their reputations to hire me as an assistant—beginning in college. I am grateful to Rev. Guy Rayle, Rev. Buddy Rampey, Dr. Eugene Cockrell, Rev. James Denny, Dr. Dan Reiland, and Dr. John Maxwell.

Dr. Steve Babby was my mentor for many years. I am forever indebted to him for the hours he invested in me.

I would never have entered the ministry without the influence of my parents, Rev. Ralph and Marguerite Westafer. Born with a birth defect, I was treated like the rest of their children. I was always accepted and loved. Even though they pastored small churches during their time on earth, they were faithful servants and loved by their congregations.

Thanks to all the churches I served over the decades. I

owe a debt of gratitude to the First Baptist Church of Cowpens, South Carolina, for sticking with me. We've been through peaks and valleys for more than ten years, but you will always have a special place in my heart for what you've done for me.

To my wife, Patti – thank you for waiting. I am so thankful for your constant encouragement. God brought us together providentially. You believed in this project and I am so blessed you believe in me. I love you.

Introduction

I knew something was up when I walked into the auditorium for the second service and everybody was looking at me with Cheshire grins. People who attended the first service were back for the second. The auditorium was packed. We were ushered to the platform in front of the puppet set adorning the stage.

Focus on the Family had launched a new initiative known as "Pastor Appreciation Month." My California church took it seriously. As we sat, suddenly about twenty puppets appeared behind us. The Ray Boltz' sound track of *Thank You* began and I wept uncontrollably as a friend sang such a wonderful song of appreciation, accompanied by a cadre of puppets.

As the song concluded, the theme song to *Hawaii Five-O* blared on the speakers and two life-sized puppets in hula skirts, Hawaiian shirts and leis came sprinting down the aisle.

The crazy puppets could barely contain themselves as they made the announcement. Our wonderful, loving, supportive church presented us with an all-expense paid trip to Hawaii! I was overcome with emotion as the congregation clapped and cheered.

That's the way churches should feel about their pastor. I still am moved when I think about the wonderful people who gave sacrificially to show their appreciation.

Years later, I accepted a call to an urban church in the Midwest. It was a wonderful opportunity with a church full of potential. It also moved us closer to my parents since my father was battling illness.

It took only two weeks before the first church crisis arose. It was a financial situation created before I ever arrived. We did our best to resolve it, but it was only the beginning of constant waves of toxic issues battering the church like a tropical storm.

There were tensions with the worship. We had a traditional service in the sanctuary and a non-traditional service in the new gym. Each service had a different leader and a different style. Not long after the financial crisis, the leader of the non-traditional service resigned. He and his family were leaving the church because of the way some treated his wife.

There was constant conflict with the church and the school it hosted. The school administrator resigned in the middle of the school year.

A staff change aggravated those loyal to the former staff member. A new approach to a long-standing financial tradition was proposed by some board members and I was stuck in the middle. When presented to the congregation, it was summarily defeated.

It was one battle after another. I was having nightmares about people chasing me, wanting to trap me and kill me. The continuous church conflict was negatively affecting my family.

Within fourteen months of moving across the country, I resigned. The same night, I slept like a baby.

I was the same person and pastor, but was perceived and treated differently. The first church loved me and encouraged me. In such an environment, I flourished. The second church, not so much, and I grew sullen, exhausted, and quit.

Rev. Greg Laurie has said, "Don't waste your pain." I determined to use both my positive and negative encounters as a pastor to help you.

From my experiences and those of others you will meet in this book, I discovered commonalities which contribute to clergy stress. These events or circumstances can break a pastor.

There is hope! I learned how a pastor can reduce the effects of clergy stress. By applying some simple practices, the quality of life for a pastor can improve remarkably. In addition, such practices may also improve the chances for a pastor to have a longer tenure at a church.

As in anything else in life, the decision and choices are up to you. My prayer for you is for God to use this book to better your life and ministry.

Bill Westafer, Ed.D.

CHAPTER 1

Trial by Fire

"If the other man's grass is always greener,
think of his fertilizer bill."

"God told me He was gonna kill that baby!" The sudden outburst from a jealous woman in the congregation left the pastor dumbfounded as he stood in the pulpit. She had stalked this young pastor for months. She wrote unflattering letters to his pregnant wife. Just a moment earlier, he tearfully confided to his congregation his young wife miscarried on Saturday. Now the female stalker stood in a service with the vulnerable target of her affections in her sights for a public proclamation of why she should replace the pastor's wife. All the while, the congregation tolerated the abhorrent behavior of a woman bent on destroying the pastor's marriage.

Fights, fires and fools have been a part of the church long before the 21st Century. Toxic behavior makes the pastoral ministry one of the most stressful occupations in existence.

Any pastor who tells you he doesn't experience stress is either lying or will have a seat next to the Boanerges brothers at the marriage supper of the Lamb. James and John, the Sons of Thunder, wanted to call down fire from heaven on a Samaritan town because the occupants didn't welcome Jesus (Luke 9:51-55). Jesus rebuked the boys and they moved to another village. Thousands of pastors do the same when they no longer feel welcome.

Some pastors fan the flames of their own stress by their ignorance, impertinence or impatience. In many instances, foolish parishioners start church fights and fires by their self-centered actions and insensitive words.

The cumulative effects can cause a pastor to lose perspective. The prophet Elijah who confronted an evil king, spent time in the desert drinking from a muddy creek, and prayed down the fire of God. When he was threatened by Jezebel, it all became too much to bear. Alone on the mountain with God, a minister is often tempted to say, "I have had enough, Lord" (I Kings 19:4).

All servants of God want to hear Jesus say, "Well done, good and faithful servant" (Matthew 25:14-23). Many pastors often hear the words of hardened, ungodly church leaders sarcastically say, "Stick a fork in him; he's done." Once more, another pastor and his family load their belongings into a moving van in search of another parish or is so disheartened he or she leaves the Call in the rear-view mirror.

Lurking like molten lava under the dome of a volcanic mountain are those waiting for an opportune moment to burn to ashes the dreams or efforts of God's called. Some parishioners feel it's their "call" to make life difficult for clergy. They call to mind flame-throwers in the military. Comedian George Carlin once opined, "The very existence of flame-throwers proves that some time, somewhere, someone said to themselves, 'You know, I want to set those people over there on fire, but I'm just not close enough to get the job done." Sometimes camouflaged, but oftentimes outspoken, flamethrowers can prove to be vocationally fatal for the clergy-person ill-prepared or uninformed on how to mediate such a hazard. Greenleaf (1) labels the likes of these as an "anti-leader." They choose only to "denigrate leadership."

Seventy percent of pastors say they have lower self-esteem today than when they started in the ministerial profession (2). In some instances, shepherds and their flocks appear to be constantly at odds while unresolved tensions linger. Friedman (3), among others, characterized this as the triangles at work in churches.

How does a church triangle work? Consider the philosophy of my late cousin-in-law. He lived with his family in the mountains of North Carolina, where he worked for many years as a plant engineer. We were guests in their home several times and I wanted to show my appreciation for their hospitality by mowing the yard. After repeated fruitless attempts to start his mower, I called for help. The engine wasn't getting fuel. Our host bent down on his hands and knees, placed his lips over the primer bulb and blew.

"Now give it a yank." I pulled the cord and the engine roared to life. I laughed in amazement.

He deadpanned, "All an engine needs is fuel, oxygen, and a spark."

My Grandpa was born during a two-week revival at his mother's church in Goblesville, Indiana. Goblesville is so small the town square is a triangle. My great-grandmother took my newborn grandfather to the revival. He attended the same church until his death. In fact, the church changed denominations twice during his lifetime, but Grandpa kept going until his funeral. The long-time members represent the oxygen. The first ingredient or leg of the triangle in many churches is long-time members whose families comprise the hierarchy of the congregation or the "I was here first" crowd.

Unless a minister plants a church, he or she is generally considered the "traveling medicine man." In 2009, I moved to South Carolina to assume the pastorate of a 131-year-old church. Forty-two pastors and interims served four years or less. The average tenure was a little over three years. Fifteen of the pastors or interims served one year or less. When churches change pastors so frequently, he or she is viewed as transient. This position symbolizes the spark.

The third leg of the triangle is comprised of the new faces in the congregation. They seek assimilation into the worship community and wish to assume leadership or are anxious to serve. Thus, they may be characterized as fuel. When disagreements arise, personalities clash, or one leg feels threatened by another segment of the triangle, the mixture of fuel, a spark, and someone putting their lips on the primer bulb create combustion.

I saw this first-hand in an urban church I pastored in the Midwest. Located in a neighborhood whose demographics were changing dramatically, if new initiatives and new people were not introduced, the church was likely to die a slow and painful death.

Andrew* (name changed), his wife, and two teenage sons were exactly the kind of fuel this church needed. Andrew, a creative leader, was instrumental in starting an alternative morning worship service. His wife and teenage sons were involved as well.

Andrew and I went to lunch and he dropped a bomb.

"Pastor, we've decided to leave the church."

"Why?" I asked, assuming it was my fault, "Did I do something or say something to offend you?"

"No, I'm leaving because my wife can't take it anymore."

"What's going on?"

"There are women in the church who are just cruel to my wife. They say unkind things to her. They don't want her involved in ministry. I don't think a woman should come home from church in tears on Sunday because of what other women said to her."

The women who mistreated Andrew's wife weren't from the "old guard." They were flamethrowers close to her own age threatened by her passion and energy.

When I finished cutting the grass in the engineer's yard, I tried to stop the mower engine, but to no avail. Once again, I called the cousin. Without missing a beat, he grabbed a fishing pole leaning against the basement wall. Reaching the tip under the carburetor of the engine, he flipped a lever and the mower stopped immediately. When a congregation combusts, it would be nice if every pastor was equipped with a leadership fishing pole.

After serving my first ten years in the ministry as a staff pastor, I accepted the lead pastor position in a small southern

California church. "Lead pastor" is an oxymoron. "Remnant pastor" might be a better term since the congregation was only about fifty souls. We entered the stale air of a church on the brink of closing its doors. With energy, creativity, love, and lots of prayer, the spark God birthed in us spread like a California brush fire to the members of the church.

Excited about our collective future, they blew on the primer bulb and pumped oxygen into the outreach programs. They invited friends and family members. The newly assimilated people, in turn, invited their friends and family. Within a few years, the church was aflame with enthusiasm and growing. God showed up because we wanted Him and each other. It's possible for the fire of God to fall and set a church aflame for the right reasons.

It's important to differentiate two different kinds of stress. Eustress is necessary stress. It's the kind used when you lift weights or engage in cardiovascular training. Eustress is positive stress required to help you grow and improve. Distress, on the other hand, can be dangerous. Episodes of distress which are extensive or high in intensity can be damaging physically, mentally, emotionally, and spiritually.

Distress can be caused by the death of a spouse, friend or loved one. Divorce, marital separation, and arguing with your spouse can ramp up the stress level in your life. Two husbands are talking:

  "My wife drove my car and got water in the carburetor."

  "Where's the car now?"

  "In the lake."

Lack of purpose, losing a job, major physical problems and financial reversals can complicate our lives. Working constantly with no day off or vacation, or breaks wears on you. Conflicts with church members, building projects, staff hiring, firing, and evaluations can apply pressure. Having to relocate, sell a house, buy a house, foreclosure or facing retirement can all be reasons for your blood pressure to spike.

All clergy want to hear those words from their heavenly Father when they arrive at heaven's gate, "Well done, good and faithful servant." I don't believe God intended His prophets to look like a piece of charred toast upon arrival.

Pastor Hank* (name changed) longed to be mentored by an older, successful pastor. He admitted he hadn't been able to find one who was still "vibrant." While medical doctors, educators, coaches, and business people are still sought for advice well into their senior years, too many pastors are abandoned by both their congregations and their colleagues depleted of their early passion while their useful experience and expertise is ignored. The flamethrowers take their toll.

Stress as a malady is common among American society

in general and professionals in particular. Hart (4) describes stress as primarily a biological phenomenon resulting from too much adrenaline and too much pressure. An individual is using too much energy to perform certain functions. "Stress is the loss of fuel and energy that often produces panic, phobic, and anxiety-type disorders." A pastor has to shift at a moment's notice from administrative duties to the emotional and spiritual work of ministry. Since ministers are in a serving profession, many come to them as a first resource. As much as pastors entered the profession to minister to needy souls, excessive involvement in the help provider role has been shown to be a source of major occupational stress for clergy (5).

One professional stress is moving from one town to another. Anderson and Stark (6) referred to repeated job relocation as "mobility syndrome." Stress manifested from this includes depression, marital discord, loss of support networks, interruption of personal growth and development. They further intimated teenagers in the home may be negatively affected due to impaired social relationships.

The quakes in the pond of mobility may impact the spouse who must resign a job he or she loves as a result of a new church assignment and ensuing relocation. This ripple may diminish the family's revenue stream.

Children must adjust to new schools and make new

friends. My father, for example, served as pastor in three different towns during my formative years. I was a student in three different school districts before graduating high school. I started as a Rambler, became a Golden Eagle and finished as a Dragon. The change in school colors wrought havoc on my teenage wardrobe.

The final relocation took place between my sophomore and junior years of high school and translated into a tremendous personal loss for me. During my sophomore year, my cross-country team went undefeated during the regular season and advanced deep into the post-season. When my father chose to resign and move to a new parish it meant I missed the opportunity to join my teammates the next year in a successful season and competing in the state finals. It also meant moving to a new town, a new school, and trying to make new friends, again. A teenager trying to crack well-established cliques is about as easy as trying to climb Mt. Everest without oxygen.

Since many pastors live in church-provided housing as part of their financial package, they miss the benefit of building home equity. The economic pressures to prepare for retirement, achieve home ownership, and provide a stable environment for a family can be jeopardized by frequent moves. My father pastored smaller churches and we always lived in a parsonage manse. This was considered part of the salary package and, in turn, made it difficult for my parents to save enough for a down payment on a house. This was exemplified by an experience my parents never shared with me until more than twenty years after it occurred.

Called to pastor a struggling church of fifty parishioners in the early 1970s, Dad worked second jobs to make ends meet. The church couldn't afford much in the way of salary, but did provide a nice parsonage. What I didn't learn until nearly two decades later was the vacation policy of the church. When we took a week of vacation, my father was required to pay the stipend for his replacement speaker. Imagine the utter insanity of such a practice in the world of business. Who would choose to work for such an organization which required anyone to pay their replacement while on vacation?

A second category of stress for professionals is related to role expectations and time demands. Quick, Nelson, and Quick (7) noted the "two major sources of stress for an executive are internal and external demands." Internal demands represent the personality and the self-imposed pressures to achieve promotions or achieve specific social status. External demands include external elements such as customers, interpersonal demands, informational demands, and personal demands. This is similar to the triangle of forces a pastor may face in a combustible church. One CEO characterized these demands "like being the center of an hourglass" where the "pressure pours in" through the top from the board with the leader in the middle and the "open funnel at the bottom pouring out" to everyone else (8).

One church I pastored had a long tradition as a major missions donor in the denomination. Financial pressures were causing some on the church board to dial back our missions giving. At the board meeting prior to the church conference, the leaders decided to reduce the missions giving goal. One board member said he would be the spokesperson since it was such a delicate issue.

A respected denominational official who was also a member of our church came to my office because he'd gotten wind of the board's decision. He told me he wasn't in favor of the decision, but he wanted me to know this in private. He would not say anything at the church conference.

Prior to the conference, the board member who offered to make the presentation on the missions cut-back changed his mind. It was left to me to present this to the congregation. I'd barely been at the church a year. When I presented the recommendation, the denominational official stood and gave an impassioned plea not to change our budget. All the board members were silent. I was left twisting in the wind.

A third classification of professional stress is the lack of social support. Marshall and Cooper (9) believed the two most important dimensions as far as the manager and his or her work are concerned appear to be those of time management and social support. The research of Quick, Nelson, and Quick (10) indicated of all the stress prevention techniques suggested by executives, "social support was the one strategy which they argued for vigorously and adamantly." What complicates this for executives is the often-transient nature of their lifestyle and their relocation to new neighborhoods. Ammons et al. (11) posited "one reason members of the community do not reach out to its new members is that they realize many of them will move again in a short time period, and therefore do not think it prudent to become involved with them either civically or socially." This sounds like the conflicted parishioner who tells his pastor, "Look, Preacher, you can always move somewhere else. I have to stay and live with these people."

The combination of pressures from unrealistic expectations, parish and family demands; member migration, professional comparisons, dysfunctional people, loneliness, and financial pressures; along with the ordinary mandates of life, makes the ministry seem as desirable a vocation as being a test dummy for bullet-proof vests. Even though these nemeses may be common to other professions, they are multiplied for clergy because of the pressure to live exemplary lives as a standard for others. R. M. Oswald wrote, "In my early years as a parish pastor, migraine headaches, an upset stomach, fatigue and depression were my daily bread and butter. Today, things are different, to be sure, but I still have difficulty managing the work and responsibility I undertake" (12).

The cumulative effect of these pressures led to my exit from pastoral ministry after nearly two decades. Reeling from fourteen months of constant fire fights and crises, attacks directed at my family, and the territorialism of church politics, I resigned to pursue other career options. Seven years later, I embarked on research to seek insight into this troubling pattern among pastors and the heat-seeking missiles launched against them. In 2009, I returned to the pastoral ministry. My church recently celebrated my tenth anniversary. I am now the second-longest tenured pastor in her history.

Consider three young Hebrew men, refugees in a foreign country. They had no idea God would place them as a leg in a political triangle God used for His glory. In Chapter 2 of Daniel, the prophet describes the ninety-foot golden image King Nebuchadnezzar, the monarch of Babylon, built.

Anyone who didn't bow to the golden image would be thrown into a blazing furnace. This already sounds like a church fight.

Shadrach, Meshach and Abednego, probably in their

mid-thirties, would've been in the king's service for several years. They had to choose between their allegiance to God or Nebuchadnezzar. Will you bend to the desires of men or will you honor the will of God when you're tried by fire?

After nineteen years of conquest, Babylon was a melting pot of nations knit together under one empire. The gathering before this image was designed to unite the empire and eliminate any disloyalty. It was a festive occasion, at least in the mind of Nebuchadnezzar. Specific instructions were given. When the musicians started playing, everyone present was to bow toward the statue. Accordingly, everyone bowed like one giant wave except Shadrach, Meshach, and Abednego. Some jealous Nellies couldn't get to Nebuchadnezzar's throne fast enough (vv. 9-12). Thus, we see the third leg of the triangle. These pure-blooded Babylonian astrologers were part of the "We-were-here-first-crowd." When they came before the king, Daniel records they "denounced" (NIV) the Hebrews. The literal translation of the Hebrew is, "ate the pieces of."

Nebuchadnezzar had a dying cow fit. This was treason! The three Hebrews are brought before him. How can they defy him after their faithful service over the years? "Is it true, Shadrach, Meshach, and Abednego, that you do not serve my gods or worship the image of gold I have set up (v. 14)?" He respected them enough he offers them a second chance accompanied by an off-hand challenge to their Jehovah, "What God will be able to rescue you from my hand (v. 15)?"

What do you do in a stressful situation which calls for you to violate your conscience? Of all the people present, 99.9% asked, "Which way do we bow?"

First, they refused to defend themselves (v. 16). This conflict wasn't about them, but God's sovereignty over their lives. Many times pastors under duress will seek to defend themselves in a church battle. God wants us to trust Him. He called you there. The place of His calling is the place of His keeping. If you have to do the wrong thing to stay on the team, you are on the wrong team.

Second, they affirmed their faith in God to deliver (v. 17). Only two things limit God's power; one of which is His character. God will never violate His attributes. In addition, God's purpose is the over-arching fact in the stress of life.

Nebuchadnezzar promptly condemns the three Hebrew stalwarts. Verse nineteen says his attitude toward them changed. Sound like anyone in your church?

The king orders the furnace, probably used to melt the gold on site, heated seven times hotter. Gold melts at 1850 degrees. Increase the temperature seven times and those boys would be instant Hebrew hash browns. Nebuchadnezzar orders the strongest soldiers to bind the Hebrews so there's no chance for them to escape.

Rather than worry, they waited. Shadrach, Meshach, and Abednego never whined. They walked in peace and power. The fire was so hot the strong men who heaved them in were killed instantly (v. 22). What went through the minds of those three Hebrew men when they weren't delivered from the fire?

Living by a worldly value system produces emptiness. Oswald Chambers once said, "Can you trust Jesus Christ where your common sense cannot trust Him?"

The king exclaimed, "Look! I see four men walking around in the fire, unbound and unharmed, and the fourth looks like a son of the gods" (v. 25). Three truths are apparent in this pagan's powerful declaration. First, Jesus was already in the fire! If you're in the midst of a stressful situation looking impossible to resolve, Jesus is beside you in the crucible of your fiery ordeal. Second, even the ungodly will see Jesus with you. This was not only true in the Old Testament, but it was also true in the New Testament, "When they saw the courage of Peter and John and realized that they were unschooled, ordinary men, they were astonished and they took note that these men had been with Jesus" (Acts 14:13, NIV).

The king of Babylon, the most powerful monarch on earth, approached the opening of the furnace. No doubt, he had his hand over his eyes and could only get so close because of the intense heat. He shouted, "Shadrach, Meshach and Abednego, servants of the Most High God, come out! Come here" (v. 26)!

I don't think Shadrach, Meshach and Abednego jumped immediately. I think they rocked a cool, confident stroll someone exhibits when they know life is good! They emerged gloriously from the fire, but weren't burned, their hair wasn't singed, their robes weren't scorched, they didn't even smell like smoke (v. 28)!

God chose to rescue the Hebrews in the furnace, not from the furnace. Would all of us like to avoid the fire? Absolutely! Will God always spare us from the fiery trials? Remember, testing comes before promotion. Nebuchadnezzar acknowledges the convictions of Shadrach, Meshach and Abednego (vv. 28-29). Then, he promotes them (v. 30).

Ben* was stalked by a female member of his church while the congregational leaders turned a blind eye. Yet, he was preparing to celebrate his twenty-fifth year of ministry at his church, a "well done" affirmation.

Donna* dealt with both a flame-throwing matriarch and a fire-breathing patriarch in a rural clique-dominated church. In spite of them, she learned the asbestos techniques to survive such hateful tactics and was in the midst of a long and fulfilling tenure.

Evan* suffered from compassion fatigue, but

acknowledged it. Even his church leaders recognized his symptoms of stress and helped him overcome. Evan was still in his lengthy pastorate when I interviewed him enjoying a great quality of life and rave reviews from his parishioners.

Frank* watched his historic church literally burn to the ground, the act of an arsonist who was never apprehended. Like a firefighter navigating his way through a smoky, burning structure, Frank learned how to navigate stress.

It's increasingly clear the implementation of multiple coping mechanisms may largely determine not only the length of ministry in a parish, but quality of life issues. Pastors need to realize they don't need to stand in the circle of fire alone. Not being alone is part of the needed flameproof coating.

*The names of study participants were changed.

CHAPTER 2

Change

"Everything flows and nothing stays. You can't step twice into the same river" (Heraclitus).

Two construction workers took their noon lunch break on the job site. The first construction worker was about to open his lunch pail when he said, "I hope I don't have meatloaf again today. I had meatloaf on Monday, Tuesday, Wednesday and Thursday. I hope I don't have meatloaf today!"

He opened his pail and exclaimed, "I don't believe it! Meatloaf again!"

"Why don't you ask your wife to fix you something different?" asked his friend.

"I'm not married," he responded. "I pack my own lunch."

Israel needed a change. Israel's King Ahab "did more evil in the eyes of the Lord" than any previous monarch (I Kings 16:30, NIV). Ahab's legacy of sin was the result of relying on politics instead of prayer. His arranged marriage to Jezebel, a Sidonian princess, was meant to provide protection against the powers from the East. The new queen substituted Baal worship in place of the worship of Jehovah.

Even Jezebel's name was a type of mantra calling for her deity, "Where is Baal?" Even though she was described as beautiful, a portion of her name, "zebel", in Hebrew meant dung. Who would want to marry a woman, regardless of looks, whose name reminded you of cow-pies? Her tactics were meant to obstruct revival with her controlling and manipulative spirit.

Israel's king "began to serve Baal and worship him" (vv. 31-33). Even though Ahab was a Yahweh worshipper and named his sons after Yahweh, international courtesy demanded his foreign queen have a sanctuary for her own religion. Ahab blended his worship of God with the Baal cult worship to appease Jezebel. The result meant Ahab "did more to provoke the Lord, the God of Israel, to anger than did all the kings of Israel before him" (v. 33).

"In Ahab's time, Hiel of Bethel rebuilt Jericho. He laid its foundations at the cost of his firstborn son Abiram, and he set up its gates at the cost of his youngest son, Segub, in accordance with the word of the Lord spoken by Joshua son of Nun" (v. 34). It had been 500 years since the destruction of Jericho. Hiel was the contractor for Ahab, but the Word of the Lord spoken by Joshua five centuries earlier was ignored. "Cursed before the Lord is the man who rises up and builds this city Jericho; with the loss of his first-born son he shall set up its gates" (Joshua 6:26). Ahab was blind to the hand of God in Hiel's punishment.

Onto this chaotic stage, God brought His servant Elijah to be a firebrand for holy change. Change just for the sake of change is like steering your car with your feet. You might get away with it, but it's not a good idea.

Managing change isn't easy. Peter Drucker, the late leadership guru, believed the four hardest jobs in America were the President of the United States, a university president, a CEO of a hospital, and a pastor (1).

For any leader, the stress may be more intense due to the nature of his or her role in an organization. Leadership theories underscore the importance of the proper mission fit with the right leader for optimum mutual benefit (2).

Given the role of clergy not only in the church, but in the community, mission fit is essential for success. The responsibility to live an exemplary life and perform well in the profession may create enormous pressures. When a minister encounters stressors indigenous to their profession, he or she may emerge from disequilibrium as a better person and a more effective pastor. Others may see a personal or professional crisis as a trauma too great to overcome, negatively affecting their approach to the ministry or even hastening an exit from the profession.

My research revealed six major stressors (see Table 1): Change, Leadership, Conflict, Crises, Expectations, and

Loneliness. Seven participants reported resistance to change by individuals or factions.

Stressors

Change	Leadership	Conflict	Crises	Expectations	Loneliness
Abe	Abe	Abe		Abe	Abe
Ben	Ben	Ben	Ben		
Chet	Chet	Chet	Chet		Chet
Donna	Donna	Donna		Donna	
				Evan	
Frank	Frank	Frank	Frank	Frank	
Gwen	Gwen	Gwen	Gwen	Gwen	Gwen
Hank	Hank			Hank	Hank

(Table 1)

Unless a pastor plants his or her own church, he or she begins as the "Traveling Medicine Man" in an entrenched population with a real or implied hierarchy and established traditions. In the interview process, prospective pastors often convey to the search committee not only their qualifications, but their vision for ministry. Congregations may give the impression in the courtship phase they want a leader who will implement necessary changes for the church. When the candidate is invited to assume the pulpit, he or she may cling to the notion the congregation is ready to embrace new initiatives. However, any pastor seeking to move the congregation in a newly-defined direction or introducing an agenda agitating the status quo is likely to encounter resistance. A volunteer-intensive organization like a church is sensitive to change.

Jeff Iorg (3) lists four common mistakes pastors make with change:

1) Introducing change for the wrong reasons. This includes making the current church like the pastor's last church or copying another successful church.

2) Changing too frequently.

3) Change failing to produce the intended results.

4) Introducing self-serving change masked as a means of church improvement. This happens when a pastor tries to reinvent the church to be a certain style instead of trying to connect with the community.

As I interviewed pastors, managing change was the perfect tinder to ignite a church fire. Ministers grow frustrated if they hold unrealistic expectations for a congregation (4).

As the entrenched authority, King Ahab wasn't about to change. Neither was Queen Jezebel. They were perfectly content with the established tradition of Baal worship for the Israelites.

Change or transformation is at the core of Christianity. Paul wrote, "And we, who with unveiled faces all reflect the Lord's glory are being transformed into his likeness with ever-increasing glory, which comes from the Lord" (II Corinthians 3:18). Yet, change emerged as a stressor with the research participants for three reasons: a) the pastor didn't gain the proper consensus among the congregation, b) the pastor lacked the necessary support from influential members or c) the pastor made a premature decision to force a new initiative.

A pastor needs to realize just like his people, he or she carries a bucket of water in one hand and a bucket of gasoline in the other. Any pastor can light a fire or extinguish one.

Abe was excited about his new charge, but the search committee didn't disclose the history of their numerous church splits. The church repeated the same pattern:

1. Grow until incumbent members feel threatened.

2. Incumbent members threatened by growth make demands of the new pastor.

3. The new pastor doesn't submit and insecure members exit.

4. The offerings suffer; the disenfranchised pastor resigns.

5. The disgruntled members return.

Abe's excitement grew when sixty-seven new people

attended the church in a six-month span, until the long-time members resented the infusion of strangers. Remember the congregational triangle and the elements for a fire: established members, new members, and the pastor. Abe's assessment was "a lot of the fighting was how we were going to assimilate these people. They didn't want to grow because they were going to lose their influence in the church." Abe was frustrated when the leaders wouldn't cooperate with his attempts to try new programs. "I'd say, 'What's your plan?'

'Well, we've never done that here.'"

Chet was hired as a staff pastor at a ninety-year-old church just prior to the senior pastor's resignation. After a fruitless pastoral search, the church board decided to offer Chet the senior pastor's position.

"I knew going in they had some of those inward-focused issues they were ...not willing to deal with," he said. The previous senior pastor initiated a "re-focusing" discussion of the church's mission so it could become more effective in its outreach. As Chet tried to address the "re-focusing" issues with the church gatekeepers, some "were emphatic: 'I'm not going to change.'"

Donna, Frank, Gwen, and Hank had all been or were going through building projects. The demand for capital funds translates into sacrificial giving on behalf of the congregation.

Some may not support the project, but may choose to remain part of the congregation either stoking the fires of discontent or opting for a free ride while the project is accomplished.

A church was having a business meeting to decide whether or not to buy a chandelier for the main entrance. One of the negative gate-keepers stood and protested: "I'm against it for four reasons: One, we don't need it. Two, we can't afford it. Three, nobody here can play it. Four, what we really need is more light in here!"

Construction decisions may include everything from the style of door handles to automatic flush urinals. Members may allow individual personal preferences for color or décor to take precedence over the common good and then withhold pledges, resign from offices, or leave the church if they don't get their way.

The first church I served as pastor was still reeling from the effects of such a decision. One family left the church after they donated a used black sink for the renovation of the nursery. Common sense would dictate a remodel shouldn't include a used lavatory fixture, much less a black one. Nevertheless, the family was offended when the church leaders declined their gift. The family didn't want the sink in their home anymore, but they were insulted because the church declined it.

A former pastor may choose to retire, but continue to

attend the church. Frank dealt with this very situation. He tried to establish himself in his new responsibilities, but with the previous preacher present, the congregation was confused. People were torn between their love of the former minister and the need to give Frank an opportunity to succeed.

The predecessor was unabashed in wielding influence. "He would show up throughout the week…pumping the secretary for information…and I didn't realize it was a direct pipeline on what went on or what I stated that I thought was confidential," said Frank. He confessed, "The congregation was going through a rough time the first six months."

The former pastor died suddenly at Christmas time. His wife eventually stopped attending the church, but Frank said, "Of course [she] always kept her contacts." Frank attempted new initiatives, but they were often undermined by the widow even though she wasn't always present. Frank was frustrated, "Change was not an operative word, but a lot of people tried to run things so it was hard to get effective change to take place." Even though Frank's tenure lasted eighteen years, "I think if I would have stayed another year, it would have killed me because my vision and the way they wanted to go were two different directions and I was getting at the end of my rope."

An immature youth pastor hired by Gwen caused constant turmoil. "I would spend a lot of time putting out his fires, making him look good." An influential family in the church grew sympathetic to the youth pastor and would often defend him despite his repeated mistakes.

After eighteen months, he resigned. Gwen was relieved she wouldn't have to terminate him, but the next week he changed his mind and wanted to stay. "I was too soft. I let him stay." The next week "the whole youth group and myself and anybody else on his list got an email on a Saturday night" indicating he was resigning and wouldn't be at church the next morning. She sighed, "Almost immediately the rumors started going I forced him out." Influencers who constantly defended the youth pastor kept the gossip mill spinning.

For example, Gwen's fifty-year-old husband offered to finish the last five months of the church year as the youth pastor. She fumed, "That fueled the flame this was a conspiracy and not only had I made his [youth pastor's] life miserable," but her husband had designs on the youth pastor's position at his advanced age. She lamented, "It just killed us people were listening to this garbage."

Influential gatekeepers may feel threatened by change and criticize the pastor. If long-time members see a pastor as the "Traveling Medicine Man" in their community, they are less likely to support change.

A few years ago, a group of younger men in our church

were inspired to create a "Man Cave" class. They transformed an old second story children's department area by painting the walls in camouflage designs, mounted deer heads and netting. Fishing rods, golf clubs and other masculine décor enhanced the theme. It was fantastic. The only thing missing was some comfortable furniture.

One man asked, "Preacher, do you think we could take some of the stuffed chairs from the older men's class downstairs and move them to the Man Cave?"

I saw no harm. These older men started together in their forties and stayed together until they moved away or passed away. The majority had done the latter. What once was a robust class of nearly twenty men was now reduced by nearly seventy-five percent. Therefore, several unused, over-stuffed chairs were available. With the best of intentions, I responded, "I don't think it's a problem. Just leave enough for the guys still in the class."

Word circulated about the unseemly act of moving chairs from the older men's classroom. One member was so incensed, he threatened not to return to the class. Another member, a precious man with whom I had a great relationship, called me: "Pastor, I understand the chairs have been removed from our class."

"Well, not all of them. We left enough for the present members."

"Preacher, the men in the class each paid for his own chair. Those chairs are supposed to stay in the class."

This man who never made a critical comment to me was clearly perturbed. I had no idea the members bought their own chairs. They were in a variety of colors, by the way, no doubt to suit the individual taste of each member.

"We are leaving enough chairs for the men in the class. The chairs we moved are staying in the church and being used in another men's class."

"Preacher, if you look on the chalkboard, you'll see a plaque. It reads, 'No furniture is to be removed from this room.'"

I was stunned. I never noticed the plaque. I offered a compromise, "I'll tell you what. Any man who wants to reclaim his chair is more than welcome to come and get it. Any of the men who have passed, their families can come and get the chair. Whatever remains can be left for the present members and the rest can be used in the Man Cave."

"That's okay, Pastor. I guess it'll be okay." We parted on good terms.

After our phone conversation, I made my way into the men's class. Sure enough, there was a bronze plaque with capital black letters: "NO FURNITURE IS TO BE REMOVED

FROM THIS ROOM." I promptly retrieved a screwdriver and removed the sign. No one missed it and no one has asked for it. Some of the old chairs stayed and some were moved to the Man Cave.

Kotter (5) believes there are certain priorities a leader needs to implement change successfully. These include establishing a sense of urgency, creating a guiding coalition, communicating a vision, removing obstacles to the new vision, creating short-term wins, and anchoring the changes in the corporate culture.

Wheaton identified structural constraints as a source of chronic stress in a social structure which is exactly what a pastor must overcome: the "*disjunction* between shared goals and means to achieve goals" (6). If Kotter and Wheaton are accurate in their views of change in an organizational structure, then Abe and Ben were contrasts in successfully implementing change as each encountered resistance.

Establish a Sense of Urgency

Both Abe and Ben worked like their hair was on fire. Abe's church needed finances to survive while Ben's congregation needed a larger facility to accommodate the growing crowds and replace an inadequate building. The adversity Ben encountered spanned three years and slowed his efforts to cast the vision for the congregation to relocate. For Ben, the church relocation was a metaphor: "They didn't know they were voting not only to change location, but to change their mindset."

The F. W. Woolworth Company launched in 1879, a pioneer in see-and-touch merchandising. By 1913, their success inspired the founder to build a skyscraper in New York City for their headquarters and paid for it in cash. Woolworth's hung on until the mid-1990s as one of the last five-and-dime retail stores. By 1993 almost half the 800 stores were scheduled for closure due in part to two factors: the struggling economy and its failure to let go of the past. Today, the F. W. Woolworth Company is nothing but a footnote in history.

A church can be mired in irrelevancy if a pastor can't properly communicate a sense of urgency for change while allowing the congregation to process it. Drive through some communities and see empty church buildings converted into antique stores or storage buildings because the congregation failed to grasp the urgency of change.

Create a Guiding Coalition

Trust comes by investing in the lives of people and performing competently. A pastor must communicate respect for the past and the traditions he inherits while offering change as an extension of the congregation's legacy.

The first place a pastor should build relationships is with key gate-keepers. Every organization has its gate-keepers. Ask for their input. Enlist their help and build your coalition. If they are hesitant, be willing to "duck hunt." Keith Drury, an early mentor of mine, taught me duck hunters use shotguns, not rifles to bring down their prey. Since ducks are moving targets, hunters need ammunition with a wide spray. Not all the pellets hit the duck, but enough do the trick to bring home dinner. Pastors don't need to get everything on their list, but they can achieve success if they are willing to make concessions for the greater good.

Ben didn't build consensus initially and his future was somewhat tenuous. Influential members were comfortable with the familiar and resisted Ben's attempts to improve the church's situation. Prior to his arrival, Ben's congregation was isolated and insulated and limited in its outreach. Ben determined to change their outlook and facilitate numerical growth by reaching new people. As he discipled new members and moved them gradually into leadership positions, he also won the hearts of the congregation at large. He invested time with individuals and families by building relationships.

Communicate Vision

While he emphasized soul winning and saw an influx of more than sixty new people, Abe was unable to help the incumbents see the value without feeling threatened and the new people weren't effectively assimilated into roles of leadership. The old-timers failed to grasp how the influx of newcomers would make any difference except create longer lines for the potluck.

Ben effectively articulated not only a change in location, but a change of "mindset" for outreach. He illustrated this by the way the previous church building had been repaired. Rather than do renovation projects room by room or for the entire facility, things were done piece meal and the physical appearance suffered. They moved from need to need instead of possessing a plan.

Ben cast the vision for a facility in a new location as a focal point for community ministry. This ministry center would meet the needs of people of all ages. The center would create quality student ministries and eventually include a Christian school. When I interviewed Ben, his vision had been fulfilled. After twenty-five years of community impact, his church was preparing to launch a new school.

Remove Obstacles to the Vision

Ben was a human bulldozer removing debris in the way of his vision. He supported his vision with successful fundraising while Abe alienated key influencers. Instead of convincing the leaders in his church to buy into his vision, Abe fired them from leadership positions.

The President of High Point University, Nido R. Qubein (7), once described his conversation with a naval aviator. The officer explained many pilots died because they stayed with disabled aircraft. They preferred the familiarity of the cockpit to the unfamiliarity of the parachute, even though the cockpit was a deathtrap. The trick to "buy in" for many people is moving them from the comfort of the cockpit if the plane is going down in flames.

In Concord, Massachusetts, a grave holds the bodies of five British soldiers who died in the Revolutionary War. Below their names, the gravestone says, "They came three thousand miles…to keep the past upon the throne." People resist change for any number of reasons. First, there may be a misunderstanding of the vision. Second, the fear of the unknown or the repercussions of the change may not be communicated well. Third, the trade-off may not seem worth the inconvenience. Fourth, some people may refuse to adopt a new vision simply due to pure stubbornness, negative attitudes or lack of respect for the leader.

Create Short-term Wins

Ben used a visual aid illustrating the amount of funds being raised for the new building. Therefore, the people could see tangible progress each week and celebrate. In addition, Ben's people witnessed the evidence of changed lives in the community as a direct result of their new ministry emphasis.

My own early experience taught me the best friend of any pastor alongside the anointing of the Holy Spirit is momentum. Momentum is created by short-term wins.

My first church had two plywood bins in the parking lot. When I asked the purpose of these wooden eyesores, I was told they were used to collect aluminum cans for recycling. The revenue would pay for a new roof on the parsonage.

Do you have any idea how many aluminum cans it takes to pay for a new roof? One day, a transient was walking by one of the bins and helped himself to two bags of cans. One of our church members witnessed the thief and chased him to retrieve two dollars' worth of aluminum.

Additionally, the church stashed stacks of newspapers in a barn for a paper drive. The profits from the paper were also to help pay for the new roof. By the time I arrived, neither the aluminum cans nor the newspapers were a fruitful solution to the roof fund.

We removed the plywood bins. I don't even know if anyone took the aluminum cans to the recycling center for the cash. The newspapers were carted to the paper plant and we received less than $90. We then created a progress chart with blank shingles on a roof. As people pledged and gave, the blank shingles were filled. It didn't take long for the church to raise the needed funds and get another short-term win under their belts. Any perceived loss of tradition or comfort may be offset by momentum created with short-term wins. Winning becomes part of the new culture.

Anchor Changes in the Corporate Culture

The overarching effect in Ben's church was a vibrant and growing congregation. After several years, Ben's corporate culture moved from an inwardly-focused congregation to an outward-community focus.

Change is usually a stressor while trying to motivate a congregation to accept a new direction. Knowing what to abandon, and when to abandon it, has to be practiced systematically; otherwise, change will always be impaired. Chet continued to push for the refocusing of the church's mission before the members had effectively processed the emotional toll of tragedies experienced within the congregation. Gwen introduced too much change in too short a time. Even though Hank's church doubled in attendance, he was unable to build the proper coalition to handle the added responsibilities. Every pastor would be wise to remember the German proverb, "To change and to improve are two different things."

If you're facing the daunting issue of change, you have a lot in common with Elijah. He appeared with a call from God and had a word from the Lord, "there will be neither dew nor rain in the next few years except by my word" (17:1). James described Elijah as "a man with a nature like ours, and he prayed earnestly that it might not rain; and it did not rain on the earth for three years and six months" (James 5: 17, NIV).

Elijah had his weaknesses and shortcomings. Despite his faults, he knew when a change for the spiritual good of the nation was necessary. He served the only true living God and his mission was clear: return Israel to worship only Yahweh.

Elijah spent time in prayer and was committed to his mission. It had already been dry in Israel for six months. Not only would there not be any rain, but dew wouldn't even grace the ground. Dew and rain were the two main sources of moisture in ancient Israel. Sometimes the dew would be so heavy in the mountains it seemed like drizzle. Eliminating both sources would mean a drought of epic proportions.

Ironically, Baal, the god of fertility, was supposed to be present in the dew and the rain. God's drought was a direct challenge to this alien deity. Elijah was confident of God's call. He delivered his message to the wicked King Ahab and then trusted God Almighty to deliver on His promises. A change for the good was on the horizon for Israel. Like the construction worker at the top of this chapter, if you are tired of meatloaf then it's up to you to make a change.

54

CHAPTER 3

Leadership

"He who thinks he leads when no one is following is
only taking a walk."

Elijah's development as a leader parallels a pastor's in I Kings
17. Elijah's signature moment on Mount Carmel came after he
rebuilt God's altar. To enjoy victory, he constructed his own
"Altar of Leadership" with six stones.

The Stone of Isolation

God instructed Elijah to hide in the Kerith Ravine. It wasn't the
end of the world, but you could see it from there. At the time,
Elijah didn't know this was for his own protection. Elijah would
be safe while God orchestrated Israel's drought. Kerith means
"cutting place" or "separation." The prophet would be safe from
Ahab's wrath and Jezebel's minions. The drought would be part
of God's judgment on Israel with not only a famine of food, but
the Word of God.

God needed uninterrupted time with Elijah. If Elijah
could stand the solitude, endure the oppressive heat, and wait

patiently for his airmailed meals, he could take anything. Communion with God keeps us sensitive to His voice.

While serenaded by a babbling brook in the Kerith Ravine, Elijah listened to God. As the sun grew hotter, Elijah's heart grew softer. Forged in the crucible of a deserted ravine, Elijah made better leadership decisions because of his retreat with his loving heavenly Father. Every pastor needs moments of isolation. Spiritually, you can't lead people while you leak oil. Daily time alone with God is essential.

Pastors are often guilty of choosing the elevator of success rather than climbing the stairs of process. Some hop from a small church to a larger one prematurely; lacking the necessary convictions and leadership principles developed in an obscure place. If a pastor doesn't pay his dues, he may pay the piper.

A few years ago, I toured the headquarters of the North American Mission Board of the Southern Baptist Convention in Alpharetta, Georgia. Along with a group of other pastors, I was escorted into the corner office of Kevin Ezell, the Executive Director.

Rev. Ezell directed our attention to the painting of a small, white, clapboard church positioned on the wall directly across from his desk. "That was my first church," he explained. "It came with seven members, graffiti, and a wino."

He asked if we ever watched the television show *Cops*. "If you have, that church has been on twice."

So, how did the Executive Director who coordinates the church planting for 46,000 Southern Baptist congregations secure his first appointment? "The church interviewed several candidates, but the wives of the prospective pastors refused to live in the parsonage. My wife was the first one to agree so I got the job."

After his first message on his first Sunday in his first church, one of the seven members reprimanded him. "Preacher, you forgot to take an offering. You won't last long if you don't take an offering every Sunday."

Rev. Ezell pointed towards the picture of his first church and said affectionately, "I've had that picture for years. It reminds me of where I came from and why I'm here."

The Stone of Provision

The ravens brought Elijah bread and meat in the mornings and evenings (verse 6). In the ancient world, ravens were omens of misfortune, tragedy and death. To the Hebrews, they were unclean and contaminated. Mostly, ravens ate scraps of putrefying flesh.

Along with the groceries, God provided water from the

brook, but as the drought lingered the stream grew muddier. The oppressive heat added to his physical misery. Temperatures in Gilead could easily reach 120 degrees. It was a dry and lonely place, but Elijah knew God sent him to Kerith so God would support him at Kerith.

A leader needs to know the place of God's calling is the place of God's keeping. The place of provision might not be everything we want or expect. In some cases, you may think God is sending putrefied meat delivered by disgusting ravens.

Like Kevin Ezell's first church, some pastors are forced to accept the home provided by the congregation. Our family's first should have been an amusement park ride. My mother used to joke it required a seat belt to stay on the toilet. At mealtime, we had to be ready at a moment's notice for the salt and pepper shakers to slide across the table because the kitchen floor was tilted.

After my two older sisters graduated from college, I wanted to follow suit. I broached the topic with my mother in our basement while she ironed clothes: "Mom, am I going to be able to go to college?"

"The only way you can go is if God does a miracle. The farm money is gone."

Prior to entering the ministry, my parents were farmers. Dad was saved in a small country church after returning from his service in the Navy during World War II. Shortly after his salvation, he was called into the ministry. I distinctly remember Mom and Dad holding a sale for all the farm equipment. One week, our family of six lived on a farm. The next, we were sitting in a small town church listening to my dad's first sermon.

The "farm money" helped the transition to our new life. Both my sisters married almost immediately after college and depleted the remainder of the farm windfall. With dad's salary at a small church, he couldn't pay for my education.

Even so, I hoped God would make a way. Our parents taught us as children to tithe. They drilled into us we were to give at least ten percent of everything we earned. Mom and Dad practiced what they preached and they expected nothing less from us.

My brother and I learned this lesson early when we mowed Mrs. Hoggatt's yard for two dollars a week. Dad took fifty cents to fill the gas can. My brother and I split the remaining $1.50 and I made sure I tithed off the seventy-five cents.

The last semester of my senior year, I received letters from both the state of Indiana and the federal government. In each case, I was awarded a four-year scholarship or grant. God was answering our prayers and honoring our tithes.

The first week of college, I went to the bursar's office to

check on my financial status before I started classes. "What do I owe for my first semester?"

The lady at the window pulled my file. She looked over the paperwork for an excruciatingly long time. Finally, she looked up and said the unexpected, "Bill, you have so much scholarship and grant money we had to make one of your scholarships honorary!"

I was dumbfounded! Not only did God provide for my first year of college, He provided *more* than enough, but wait—there's more!

A schoolteacher named Helen Shellenbarger was a long-time member of the small country church where Dad was saved and called into the ministry. She made a commitment to assist with college expenses for any child from her church. The first week of every semester for four years, I would go to my campus mailbox and find a letter from Mrs. Shellenbarger. I opened the envelope from this precious woman of God and found a brief note of encouragement along with a check. To my amazement, it was always enough to cover the cost of my textbooks.

The Stone of Humiliation

The brook at the Kerith Ravine went dry. God answered Elijah's prayer and now a drought was changing the landscape. The next phase had to bother Elijah, "Then the word of the Lord came to him: 'Go at once to Zarephath of Sidon and stay there" (vv. 8-9).

Zarephath, a small Phoenician town about eighty miles north of Israel, was also located in Queen Jezebel's homeland! Zarephath was the very citadel of idol worship for Baal and Ethbaal. What do you do when God asks you to do something which makes about as much sense as betting your 401K on 13 black?

The Lord told Elijah a widow in Zarephath was already strategically placed to provide his food. Ancient tradition regarding widows and orphans was strict; a man was never to impose on them. God made it clear: "Do not take advantage of a widow or orphan. If you do and they cry out to me, I will certainly hear their cry. My anger will be aroused, and I will kill you with the sword; your wives will become widows and your children fatherless" (Exodus 22:22-24, NIV). A widow was synonymous with poverty.

Undeterred, Elijah completed the eighty-mile hike to Zarephath. Overheated and tired, he couldn't remember the last time he tasted fresh water. The ravens may have followed him on the trip just waiting for him to drop. "When he came to the town gate a widow was there gathering sticks. He called to her and asked, 'Would you bring me a little water in a jar so I may have a drink?' As she was going to get it, he called, 'And bring me, please, a piece of bread'" (vv. 10-11).

Here's a widow outside the city gathering a few sticks for a final fire and a last meal. Elijah boldly asks her for water and she departs to fulfill his request. Then came further humiliation for Elijah: "As she was going to get it, he called, 'And bring me, please, a piece of bread.'" With the Mosaic guidelines in the back of his head, this was like death for Elijah. He only made the request because God called him to this place.

Zarephath means "place of refining." God used the destitute widow to finish the refining process in Elijah. Moments of humiliation are necessary because real peace is trusting God when He doesn't make any sense.

The first church interview I had to be an assistant pastor in Eden, North Carolina, didn't go well. After being grilled by the search committee, I was excused. I remember sitting alone in the church's darkened sanctuary and having a one-sided conversation with God, "What am I doing here? I have no idea why I'm here. I guess I'll look for another job tomorrow."

Just then, Pastor Rampey joined me. "Bill, let's go back to the parsonage, get a sandwich, and talk."

"Great," I thought, "let's prolong the agony." I thought it was decent of him to give me a last meal before he said, "Thanks, but no thanks."

Pastor Rampey's wife, Joan, prepared some delicious snacks and sweet tea.

"Bill," said Pastor Rampey trying his best to hide a wry smile, "we'd like to invite you to be our new assistant pastor."

I couldn't believe my ears. Pastor Rampey must have noticed my look of disbelief. "You do?" I stammered.

"Well, actually, Troy [one of the members of the search committee] said it best, 'I think he needs us, more than we need him.'"

At some point, every pastor, will probably experience some type of humiliation. Bible characters weren't exempt and we shouldn't expect anything less.

Both matriarchal and patriarchal figures gave a lot of money at Donna's parish. Both were a constant source of upheaval. As a lifelong member, the patriarch grew agitated over trivial things like measuring the distance between the folding tables and the walls for a potluck. Such members bring to mind the assessment of one Boston politician, "He could screw up a two-car funeral." Albert Einstein once said, "The difference between genius and stupidity is genius has its limits."

The Stone of Preparation

When Elijah spotted the widow, God's preparation paid

dividends - a desperate pagan widow saw God in him. "I don't have any bread," said the widow, "just a handful of flour and a little oil in a jug. I am gathering a few sticks to take home and make a meal for myself and my son so we can eat it and die" (v. 12). Even Jesus would refer to this vortex of preparation in Luke 4:25-26, "I assure you that there were many widows in Israel in Elijah's time, when the sky was shut for three and a half years and there was a severe famine throughout the land. Yet Elijah was not sent to any of them, but to a widow in Zarephath in the region of Sidon."

God chose an unbeliever to develop Elijah. Many distressed pastors may think they're leading a congregation of unbelievers when their leadership is challenged. Blume (1) reported church control was the number one reason for forced pastor terminations in Southern Baptist Churches in South Carolina.

With the exception of Evan, all the participants in my study had his or her leadership challenged. "The church is a volunteer organization, and there's no more difficult group to run" (2). Civil War general William Tecumseh Sherman found when commanding volunteers, "I never did like to serve with volunteers because instead of being governed, they govern" (3).

Leadership issues can make a pastor feel like he's been thrown into a Rottweiler pit with a pork chop tied around his neck. In my research, friction usually occurred within the first two years when congregational leaders perceived a loss of their long-held influence. Frank admitted he was not a "natural-born leader," but the demands upon him as a pastor forced him to develop his leadership skills. Over a twenty-year span at Chet's church, "between pastors and staff pastors there were twenty-one people who went through the church." Keeping the pastoral turnstile moving creates inconsistent leadership and lay people assume positions of power. Gwen didn't blame her leadership problems on being a female, but rather "people in small churches, small rural churches with too much power or maybe have too little power and want more."

When he was a self-employed businessman, Hank had to answer to only one person. The transition to leading a congregation was difficult because "having 300 people question everything you do is a stress."

Early in his tenure, Ben said the elders in his church told him directly all he needed to do was preach and teach and they'd handle everything else. He definitively stated their view of his role would need to change because he saw himself as the leader. An insubordinate group who didn't agree with his philosophy, later served as the ringleaders of an unsuccessful coup. Ben was able to survive because of lay leaders he developed.

The Stone of Conviction

Elijah spoke confidently to the widow, "Don't be afraid. Go home and do as you have said. But first make a small cake of bread for me from what you have and bring it to me, and then make something for yourself and your son. For this is what the Lord, the God of Israel, says, 'The jar of flour will not be used up and the jug of oil will not run dry until the day the Lord gives the rain on the land" (I Kings 17:13-14).

The widow was confirmation of what the Lord told Elijah. His conviction was contagious. God honored his faith concerning the drought in Israel, provided for him at the Kerith brook and God would provide through this widow in the midst of enemy territory.

It's important to note God didn't contradict His rules about widows. Elijah gave specifications, "But first make a small cake of bread for me from what you have and bring it to me" (v. 13). The widow needed to trust God's representative. "And then make something for yourself and your son." This was a huge leap of faith for this woman with possible catastrophic consequences if Elijah was a fraud.

The destitute lady only had enough for herself and her son for one last meal. How many times has a pastor gone to a new parish and it may be the last chance for a church?

The widow must have thought, "This guy has no food. He has no water. He's a complete stranger and comes in here boldly asking me to give him our last meal? I wonder if his elevator goes all the way to the top!"

Elijah assured the widow, "For this is what the Lord, the God of Israel, says: 'The jar of flour will not be used up and the jug of oil will not run dry until the day the Lord gives rain on the land'" (v. 14). God gave Elijah specific instructions on his journey. Now, Elijah gave specific instructions to a pagan widow with the force of conviction.

The Hersey-Blanchard situational model (4) suggests successful leaders adjust their styles based on the maturity of the followers. Hersey and Blanchard proposed four leadership styles: delegating, participating, selling, and telling. These styles can be adjusted as followers change and mature over time (5).

"Telling" (6) is for low maturity people who are both unable and unwilling to take responsibility to do something and are not competent or confident. This style defines roles and requires directive behavior. Abe, Chet, Gwen and Frank were forced into this approach based on the low maturity levels of their respective congregations. None of the four was able to move his or her congregation beyond this style based on the embedded traditions and entrenched hierarchy.

When the Lewis and Clark Expedition explored the

Louisiana Purchase 200 years ago, they made their way down the Missouri River, traveling from St. Louis to the Pacific Ocean. A critical moment on the two-year expedition was in Montana where they encountered a fork in the Missouri River. With no map, a wrong choice could prove fatal. The river to the right was the route the crew preferred. Captains Lewis and Clark assessed the situation and instead led their men down the left. When the team reached the massive waterfalls, Indian guides told them they would find, they all knew they chose the right way, but the leaders had to "tell" the team what to do.

"Selling" (7) is for low to moderate maturity. These people are unable but willing to take responsibility and are confident, but lack skills. Ben inherited a group with low skill sets. He not only motivated them based on his convictions, but developed the requisite skill sets in various groups to fulfill their shared vision. Donna knew the matriarch and patriarch of her church intimidated the rest of the gatekeepers. Encountering the power of these two individuals was painful, but the style of selling as she worked through her Administrative Board proved successful.

Lieutenant Colonel George Armstrong Custer, commanding officer of the U. S. Seventh Calvary, was bivouacked at Little Big Horn in southeast Montana on June 25, 1876. His effort to quell an Indian uprising resulted in the most lopsided defeat recorded by the United States military.

Sitting Bull, his counterpart, wasn't a West Point graduate or highly decorated veteran. As the leader of the disjointed Sioux nation, he was able to communicate purpose and vision.

He'd warned his people of the ensuing threat of the white man to the Sioux existence. His passion and persuasion often fell on deaf ears by tired and discouraged Sioux leaders. Undeterred, Sitting Bull turned his attention to the rising, young Sioux warriors which included Crazy Horse. He appealed to their enthusiasm, future existence, and dignity.

Sitting Bull convinced all Sioux to stand and fight in the Little Big Horn to honor their ancestors. By battling the Blue Coats on sacred ground they would draw strength from former generations. If they died, it would honor their nation's cause. If they won, they would provide hope for their future. Sitting Bull's persuasive vision won the day (8).

"Participating" (9) is for moderate to high maturity people who may be able, but unwilling to do what the leader wants. They possess a motivational problem so the leader and followers share decision-making.

God blessed the work at my first pastorate and we needed to build a new facility. We were already in two worship services. The real estate in California was phenomenally expensive, so we needed to build on our existing property with a creative solution.

A site planner recommended we raze the parsonage to make room for the new worship center, a problematic task. For one, the parsonage was a 100-year-old farmhouse with historic significance in the community. It overlooked a former orange grove in our Los Angeles suburb. In my office hung an old photograph taken from the stylish front portico of the farmhouse. It revealed a grand view of a solitary horse-drawn carriage making its way up the old dirt avenue in front of the house. The photo was undated, but it was early in the town's history.

The second difficulty was the congregation's history with the parsonage. The property was debt-free. Lots of memories were associated with the house.

Thirdly, without a parsonage, the church would have to either purchase another house or bump the pastor's pay package for a housing allowance. A collateral effect of a building program would be increasing the budget to replace a debt-free item.

As I met with our leaders, I emphasized their responsibility to meet with key influencers and learn their concerns. If the leaders couldn't find an answer, we'd get one. Our goal was a unanimous congregational vote on the site planning project.

I met with Mr. and Mrs. Fuss. Their name is really a misrepresentation because they never caused any problems. They were two of the sweetest people you'd ever meet and they loved our church.

Out of respect for their integrity and their history in the church, I made a home visit. I asked if they had any questions and they did. I went into detail about the site plan, how we'd done our research and this was the best alternative. After I addressed all of Mr. Fuss' concerns, he took a long pause which was his style when he was ready to make a decision. "Well, Pastor, if this is what you and the board thinks is the best thing to do then we will support it."

"Mr. Fuss, will you help support this with anyone else in the congregation who may have reservations?"

"I sure will, Pastor."

At our final board meeting prior to the vote, our group of leaders made a list of all the questions we'd been asked. We compiled them into an answer sheet so if there were any questions at the meeting, we would have prepared answers. I also asked Bob Lapp, the chairman of our Trustees, to present the proposal to the congregation. Mr. Lapp was a long-tenured and respected leader.

It was a packed house the day of the vote. Mr. Lapp

artfully presented our proposal. The leaders did their advance work well and there was an air of excitement in the auditorium. Only two questions were asked and each had already been addressed. Finally, the moment came for the vote. Bear in mind, this had been a traditional church oftentimes marked by dissent. This was a pivotal moment to revert to the old ways or move forward in the power of God. The vote was unanimous! Everyone was excited. It's one of the greatest moments I ever experienced as a pastor. God truly answered prayer.

As we closed the meeting, I asked Mr. Fuss to lead us in a benediction. In his own inimitable, sweet way, he affirmed this was the right decision for our congregation and prayed beautifully to close our meeting.

"Delegating" (10) is for high maturity people both willing and able to take responsibility. This level requires little direction or support. After twenty-five years and changing the culture of the congregation, Ben is now operating in this style.

This latter practice is often marked by lengthy pastorates. I witnessed this first-hand early in my career while on staff under Dr. Eugene Cockrell. Dr. John Maxwell, noted leadership guru with whom I also served in California, once said Pastor Cockrell had done one of the best jobs he witnessed developing lay leaders.

Dr. Eugene Cockrell was the founding pastor of

Lakeview Wesleyan Church. He deftly led them through numerous expansions and building programs. He left to pursue denominational opportunities for a while and then the church invited him to return after the resignation of another pastor. It was during his second tour of duty I worked with Pastor Cockrell.

I witnessed a tireless worker with a knack for spotting leaders and placing them in positions of authority. He would release and trust these people to do ministry and expand the influence and effectiveness of the church. Stan Tyner, was a long-time member of Pastor Cockrell's flock. He affectionately referred to him as a "benevolent despot." Stan illustrated this by saying Pastor Cockrell was the first pastor ever to visit him and his wife in their home after they visited Lakeview. He was always available when Stan and his family needed him, but Dr. Cockrell was also the undisputed leader of the church. The staff and laity knew he would always make the tough decisions. He loved his people, built relationships, worked competently, and built a track record of success.

The Stone of Inspiration

"She went away and did as Elijah had told her. So there was food every day for Elijah and for the woman and her family. For the jar of flour was not used up and the jug of oil did not run dry, in keeping with the word of the Lord spoken by Elijah" (vv. 15-16).

The widow's selfishness could have killed her and her son. She had to be willing to trust the word of Elijah and sacrifice her security. When congregations refuse to listen to God's man, they rob themselves of great blessings.

Taking care of Elijah gave this woman a new purpose and renewed hope. God used the widow to meet the material needs of Elijah.

Elijah's pride could have killed him. His response to the moments of instruction, provision, humiliation, and preparation built his convictions and led to inspiring others.

There were instances in my study when the leadership stress reported by pastors was self-inflicted. Adapting the right leadership style in the context of the congregation is essential.

CHAPTER 4

Conflict

"Conflict is inevitable; combat is optional" (Max Lucado).

We lived in a 100-year-old farmhouse when I pastored in Southern California. The historic house was the parsonage for our church, located on the acreage of a former orange grove. The house was a two-story structure with a root cellar under our master bedroom. The foundation was a mixture of block, brick, rocks, and wooden beams. Such construction came in handy for earthquakes. The house kind of rolled with the punches. We loved the house because it had character.

Grandpa Taylor, a long-time member of our church, would often come and trap the skunks who also found a home under our house. We knew they were under the house, not by smell, but the noises or scratching we heard. Early one morning, we were awakened by the familiar sound of scratching. Then we heard screeching. A terrific fight ensued – for about ten seconds. Then we smelled the bomb. A possum invaded the serenity of the skunk habitat and Mama wasn't happy. Our bedroom reeked. I pulled the covers tight over my eyes, mouth, and nose, but the stench was too much. We ran into the living room, but the smell permeated the ground floor.

I called Grandpa Taylor to come, please, and remove any and all critters responsible. He promptly arrived, but he could do nothing about the foul odor. We called a pest control expert to see if anything could be done to eliminate or mask the lingering rancidness. He brought a gallon concoction of orange fluid designed to negate the smell. His cure wreaked nearly as bad as the cause. Eventually, it worked and the smell subsided.

That same evening, we had an activity at church. As we filed in, people's noses started to twitch. "What's that smell?" Even though we'd taken showers, the toxicity infected our clothes and we brought it into church.

Frost (1) labeled conflict in companies "organizational toxicity." Whether it's a business or a church, it stinks. Six of the eight pastors in my interviews encountered toxic congregants bent on undermining or discrediting them. Clergy shared multiple stories of encounters with dysfunctional people, perceived threats to authority, territorialism, and contentious behavior. What amazed the preachers in this study was the ferocity with which some people acted since they were supposed to be the body of Christ. In many cases the behavior was simply boorish, immature and mean-spirited people. Surprisingly, it was usually a small cluster of people. Mismanaged or unrequited dissonance may lead to termination, resignation, or even an exit from the vocation. Gray (2) reported almost half of all terminations or pressured resignations were caused by a faction of ten people or less.

Hoge and Wenger (3) surveyed former pastors who identified the five top conflict areas as pastoral leadership, finances, changes in worship style, conflicts among staff and new building or renovation issues. Further, thirty-nine percent of the respondents in Hoge and Wenger's study had major conflicts in the last two years of their parish ministry. Gray (4) reported one psychiatrist who worked with companies downsizing and concluded corporations treat their employees better than churches treat theirs.

The prophet Elijah dealt with conflict as he fulfilled his mission. Even though he confronted King Ahab, Jezebel was the power behind the throne. Her antics in I Kings 21 parallel church fights. Not all disagreements in a church are spiritual. Pastors and congregations may experience seasons of "cyclical conflict," which is simply part of the growth process. When a church plateaus, there may be plenty of parking. When a church grows, traffic patterns emerge. Parking spaces are maxed. Somebody may lose their favorite parking space and get upset, but the influx of new faces should cause the inconvenience to be overlooked. There's an ebb and flow to a church. Cyclical issues are not cause to terminate someone or submit your resignation.

"Chronic conflicts" are kamikaze churches or "meat

grinders" who gain a reputation for "organizational toxicity." They kill the spirit of more than one preacher and their community reputation is in tatters. This kind of congregation may have a lot in common with Queen Jezebel. She was laser-focused on getting her way. She's a little like the ministerial student who graduated from seminary, but never believed in original sin. About twenty years later, he ran into one of his professors. The teacher asked if he still didn't believe in original sin. The now-seasoned pastor responded after raising teenagers and pastoring a church, he not only believed in original sin, but now he also believed in demon possession.

Naboth's beautiful vineyard had been in his family for generations. Adjacent to Ahab's summer palace, the king wanted it for a vegetable garden. Naboth was a righteous man and denied Ahab's offer to buy the property, "The Lord forbid that I should give you the inheritance of my fathers" (v. 3). His case was based on the Mosaic Law, "No inheritance in Israel is to pass from tribe to tribe, for every Israelite shall keep the tribal land inherited from his forefathers" (Numbers 36:7, NIV).

As a Hebrew, albeit a wicked one, Ahab would've known the Law but chose to ignore it. When Naboth refused his offer, the king returned to his stately surroundings and pouted. The Scripture says he was "sullen and angry" (v. 4). Even though he was the king of Israel, he "lay on his bed sulking and refused to eat" (v. 4).

J. Oswald Sanders (5) wrote, "Leadership is influence." The chief influencer for King Ahab was Queen Jezebel. She was also the key intimidator of the nation of Israel and manifested a number of ungodly traits when she locked Naboth and his inheritance in her crosshairs. The same Jezebel traits revealed in this story are often conjured when conflict arises in a church.

Jezebel Trait #1: Domination

Ahab's domineering queen fussed at him, "Is this how you act as king over Israel? Get up and eat! Cheer up. I'll get you the vineyard of Naboth the Jezreelite" (v. 7). She forged letters in Ahab's name, "placed his seal on them, and sent them to the elders and nobles who lived in Naboth's city with him" (v. 8).

Ben humorously labeled opposition as dealing with "hard-headed members" and just plain obstinate people. He remembered, "If you're going left, they're going right." In Ben's case, as he worked on a vision, strategy and mission for the church and the requisite resources and management team, he experienced conflict. "When people fight, they'll use whatever or whomever." Ben was physically threatened. "One man wanted to jump on me at one of my meetings, but it was fine. Now, of course, I'm saved, but I don't think you need to push me that far…I've had guys in my chest as a leader…I believe in turning the other cheek, but I still got some of that other stuff in me," he laughed.

Gladwell (6) characterizes this as a "culture of honor." When one family fights with another, it's a feud. When lots of families fight, it's a pattern. In the "culture of honor," an individual has to be willing to fight in response to even the slightest challenge to his reputation. Ahab started the feud with Naboth and Jezebel finished it. Naboth was polite and direct, simply stating God's promise. Through Jezebel's demonic lens, Naboth was nothing more than a mosquito about to be drawn into her bug-zapper. When it comes to the "culture of honor," Gladwell explained "violence wasn't for economic gain. It was *personal*." (p. 169). Ahab didn't need a vegetable garden. As the king of Israel, he lacked nothing, but Jezebel made this a personal vendetta. When a pastor tries to lead, he or she may very well run into a Jezebel who takes it personally. Jezebel loves power. She bristles at authority. She will make political alliances to achieve her end-game because she thinks she's always right.

Jezebel Trait #2: Hypocrisy

Jezebel's evil intentions were cloaked in a veil of spirituality.

She instructed the elders to "Proclaim a day of fasting and seat Naboth in a prominent place among the people" (v. 9). A religious spirit searches for allies. In this case, it was the elders and nobles. Jezebel even wanted them to proclaim a fast as window dressing to frame Naboth.

The "beginning of the downturn" for Gwen's pastorate took place when two influential families had a disagreement and severed relationship with each other, "but they both continued coming to the church," she said. The atmosphere in the church was unhealthy. Gwen explained, "People don't want to be in a church where there's a noticeable tension." The result was oppressive. Gwen's attempts to serve as a mediator between the two clans failed and only seemed to add more fuel to the fire.

Chet admitted he worked in an unhealthy church with "a lot of family roots deep within the church." As the old guard died off "those families were losing the grip they had for so many years." He conceded, "Every time an issue came, it was one of those families at the forefront of the fighting."

Jezebel Trait #3: Manipulation

I Kings 21:11 describes the power of the Jezebel spirit, "So the elders and nobles who lived in Naboth's city did as Jezebel directed in the letters she had written to them." She used the legalese of the Mosaic Law to get Naboth killed. She wouldn't do it; she used other people. The Jezebel spirit is persuasive, deceptive, and manipulative with them. It uses guilt to convince others God is disappointed in them. It flatters people, just to flatten them, "seat Naboth in a prominent place among the people, But…" (v. 9). She operates in confusion and chaos. She uses emotion to her advantage like pouting, shedding crocodile tears, or using the silent treatment. Many times when people are around someone operating in the Jezebel spirit, they say the same thing: "It's like walking on egg shells."

One member of Ben's congregation threatened to take "thirty percent of the congregation with him." Ben bluntly replied, "Maybe you need to leave. See you later." The man never left and Ben's assessment was "he couldn't influence thirty percent of my congregation anyway." Ben believed such people have a "narcissistic perception of themselves." One disgruntled member even called a local banker and requested the bank not loan the church any money. Reflecting on the act of the hateful man, Ben humbly intoned, "I preached his funeral. He never knew I knew he did that."

Jezebel Trait #4: Perjury

Jezebel invited the leaders of the city to conspire against a blameless man. "But seat two scoundrels opposite him and have them testify that he has cursed both God and the king" (v. 10). Anyone familiar with Naboth's character knew he was incapable of either act, but the nobles were nonplussed. They recruited a couple of "scoundrels" to publicly accuse a man with baseless charges: "Naboth has cursed both God and the king'" (13).

My interviews revealed petty examples of distortions ministers often encountered. Frank's job was threatened simply because he took his child for a stroll in the middle of the afternoon. An acerbic member thought Frank should be in his office working, not taking a few minutes from a busy day to relax with his young family. His afternoon walk was described as "negligence." Malfeasance of church funds was a false charge leveled at Ben. One of Donna's members exaggerated the amount of time she spent away from church responsibilities with her family.

Like Naboth, countless pastors have been victims of the H.A.R.M. Club: "Hit and Run Mouths." Donna was the target of animosity and internalized the pain. She developed high blood pressure and was prescribed medication. She estimated she had "about four or five people that it wouldn't make any difference what you would do. They'll bring [an issue] to the Ad Board and make a big deal out of it." At one board meeting, the patriarch "blew up and said I didn't listen to anybody." She quietly mused, "I mean it's just those little things that make you feel (she took her thumb and forefinger and made a pinching gesture) less than adequate" as her voice faded. "And that's why I say there's just a few of them, but they are the ones who are the most vocal about things. It still hurts when somebody makes a personal attack on your character."

Jezebel Trait #5: Murder

Jezebel engineered the death of a righteous man over a vegetable garden. "So they took him outside the city and stoned him to death" (v. 13). Adding to this horror, Jezebel had Naboth's sons executed (II Kings 9:26).

In 1860, an uneasy Charles Darwin confided in a letter to a friend: "I cannot persuade myself that a beneficent and omnipotent God would have designedly created the ichneumonidae with the express intention of their feeding within the living bodies of caterpillars." What appalled him fascinated entomologist William Kirby (1759-1850): The ichneumon insect inserts an egg in a caterpillar, and the larva hatched from the egg, he said, "gnaws the inside of the caterpillar, and though at last it has devoured almost every part of it except the skin and intestines, carefully all this time *avoids injuring the vital organs*, as if aware that its own existence depends on that of the insect on which it preys" (7). The Jezebel spirit often operates like the ichneumon insect. She will gnaw the insides of a church with her destructive will, leaving only a shell. Jezebel wants to suck the life from worship, fellowship, and the testimony of the church in the community.

By the time his church closed, Abe indicated he and his family "were really worn out from the fighting and dealing with the church people." He added, "It's been my experience if they can't control it then they'll gladly destroy it." Abe even took classes in church mediation and conflict resolution, but he said, "It came to the place where it's either 'You're gonna do as we say or you're gonna leave or we're gonna leave and we're never coming back and we don't care if the church burns to the ground.'" Abe's church died.

Jezebel Trait #6: Control

The wicked queen now had an open road to gain what she wanted. "As soon as Jezebel heard that Naboth had been stoned to death, she said to Ahab, 'Get up and take possession of the vineyard of Naboth the Jezreelite that he refused to sell to you. He is no longer alive, but dead'" (v. 15). In the midst of her grief, Mrs. Naboth lost her property. In Israel, if a man died with no heirs, his property reverted to the state. Jezebel knew this.

She operated in an atmosphere of instability, fear, strife and chaos with little or no regard for her victims. As a Navy SEAL, Mark Owen (8) phrased it, "An insurgency doesn't have to win. It just has to survive" (p. 117).

Gray (9) reported control topped the list of forced termination issues. He referenced the work of David Briggs who called the small faction of people who pressure a pastor or staff member to leave "clergy killers." These people are so disruptive and dysfunctional no "pastor is able to maintain spiritual leadership for long." The harm inflicted on a pastor's family, just like Naboth's, can leave scars affecting a person's attitude toward any church for years to come.

At his first church, Frank "liked 98% of them. The "two percent troublemakers" are "uncooperative." Frank went on to wryly state, "It could be the second coming of Christ and they'd take issue with the Lord and argue." Frank referred to a friend's difficulties at another church being so strenuous the pastor had a nervous breakdown. Frank was sympathetic, "Five tribes ran the congregation and there was constantly tribal warfare."

Dr. Elmer Towns, the long-time Dean of Religion at Liberty University, taught even among the most committed disciples "Things that cause people to sin are bound to come..." (Luke 17:1). Church growth can foster conflict. The key is learning to recognize and manage flare-ups. He identified seven kinds:

Territorial Conflicts: Shared leadership may deteriorate over time as one leader rises to prominence, leaving the other feeling ignored.

Border Conflicts: One deacon may be responsible for the prayer ministries of the church. Another may be in charge of the missionary program. Who's responsible for the missions' prayer meeting?

Resource Conflicts: Teachers in the Christian school begin Mondays by complaining about the mess left by the Sunday school teachers.

Ethnic Conflicts: New people become part of the congregation with different racial or ethnic values.

Influence Conflicts: The church grows and new leaders emerge. Sometimes, when people say the church is getting so big they don't know everybody any more, what they really mean is "everybody doesn't know me anymore."

Ideological Conflicts: New people in a growing church bring their own sense of what is right with them. Their views on the role of women, worship styles, and involvement in community issues can create tension.

Personality-based Conflicts: when people have a hard time just getting along with certain people.

Dr. Towns suggests four foundational principles to

resolve conflict:

1) Accurate data needs to be collected to make good decisions. Sift through everyone's feedback to discern accurately what's really happening.

2) Each person involved in the conflict needs to feel they are being treated fairly. Look for ways to achieve a win/win, not a win/lose. Listen carefully, because sometimes, the issue is not the issue. Let unhappy people speak for themselves. When someone begins "some people say," ignore such a generalization. Identify the "some" then instruct them to speak for themselves. Most of the time, "some" is code for "my opinion."

3) It's important for individuals involved in church conflict to maintain mutual respect for others. When conflict deteriorates and emotions gain the upper hand, conflict is out of control.

4) In seeking a lasting resolution to a church conflict, every effort should be made to achieve a consensus decision. It may not be the best solution, but it may be the best action for your church. Practice collaboration and if people can't participate without trying to dominate or control the church's decisions let them leave.

From 2003 to 2006, a bicentennial celebration honored the Lewis and Clark Expedition (10). This historic team was charged with finding an all-water route across North America. As a military expedition, they were noted for battles which *didn't* happen. Traveling 8000 miles across an unknown continent is an accomplishment in itself, but relying on hand signals and interpreters to avoid conflict and coexist with more than 100 nations of American Indians is nothing short of miraculous. During Lewis and Clark's first winter in the Mandan villages, Indians from hundreds of miles away came to see them. They set aside presumptions and prejudices and, for the most part, embraced each other. They were fascinated by each other's differences rather than intimidated by them.

You may be in a church right now where the spirit of Jezebel operates. Not everything should be blamed on a pastor's leadership deficiencies. Satan loves to create division in churches. An examination of the New Testament reveals such a reality in the early churches. Thankfully, Almighty God will not allow Jezebel to operate with impunity. He charged Elijah, in no uncertain terms, to confront Ahab with his sin (I Kings 21:17-23). Elijah did exactly as the Lord instructed and delivered a message of judgment. To his credit, Ahab humbled himself (I Kings 21:27-29) and the Lord gave the king a reprieve, but there is no evidence Jezebel ever repented.

Here is an all-important key: Elijah received permission from the Lord to deal with this issue. As believers, we must be careful not to engage in certain types of spiritual warfare without our Father's permission. Elijah didn't move until directed by Jehovah. In our zealousness, we may want to address the Jezebel spirit in our church or with a person, but we must be operating in obedience to the Lord. You need not be intimidated by the concept of a Jezebel spirit.

Recognize the enemies of Jezebel:

Jezebel Enemy #1: Authentic Godly Leaders

Jezebel constantly battles with people in authority. Jezebel hated Elijah and wanted to kill him. God's prophets, authentic leaders like Elijah, are pivotal to the defeat of this spirit. Jezebel hated the prophets and had them killed except for the ones Obadiah was able to save. God protected Elijah even as he lived in Jezebel's backyard.

Submit to God and resist the devil (James 4:7). It's not a person trying to intimidate you; it's a spirit. Neither Elijah, nor Elijah's successor, Elisha, ever spoke directly to Jezebel. Not even when Jezebel painted her eyes and called to King Jehu from her palace window did Jehu acknowledge her. He simply asked, "Who is on my side?" (II Kings 9:32) and commanded the eunuchs, "Throw her down!" (v. 33). Her influence or authority had to be eliminated.

Two men were sitting on a porch one summer evening. Soon a small dog came wobbling down the street and fell at the bottom of the steps in a disheveled heap. "That little dog looks awfully beat up," observed one. "Oh, that's my dog," said the other. "He comes home looking like that almost every night after he gets into fights with other dogs in the neighborhood."

"Well, he must not be much of a fighter," said the friend.

"Oh, he's a very good fighter, but he's just a very poor judge of opponents." The spirit of Jezebel is a defeated foe and no match for the power and authority of Jesus Christ! She was conquered on Calvary. In her pugnacity and pride she still thinks she can defeat God's prophets and God's people, but she is a poor judge of opponents.

Jezebel Enemy #2: The Spoken Word of God

Another enemy of this spirit is the Word of God. As you study the ministry of Elijah, you'll notice Jezebel wasn't present at Mt. Carmel. She can't and doesn't want to hear truth because it sets people free.

Jezebel Enemy #3: Prayer

Prayer binds the power of Jezebel and cripples her. Not even

Jezebel participated in her own proclamation for fasting. Prayer pries her fingers off the hearts and souls of people.

Have you thought about godly leaders who "prayed" they would die? It was largely due to depression. Moses, Jonah (4:3), and Elijah were discouraged almost to death. Such oppression must be dealt with in the proper attitude of prayer. Jesus said, "My sheep hear my voice" (John 10:27), and we do so by stopping in our tracks and listening to Him in prayer.

Jezebel Enemy #4: God Himself

Jezebel hated God. Why do you think she introduced alternative worship? She hated the grace He lavished on His people. She hated the idea God would take the lowliest to bring her down. When she met her end, two eunuchs pushed her out the window. She hated the holiness and purity emanating from God.

Jezebel Enemy #5: Repentance

She never mourned the death of her husband, Ahab, or her sin. Repentance brings the presence of Jesus. Repentance cleanses the church. Repentance establishes purity and power and defeats her spirit of control.

An Indiana church invited four former pastors to return

so the congregation could repent of sins which drove God's men away. Peter A. Joudry, pastor of Madison Assembly of God, hosted a reconciliation weekend where he and his wife washed the feet of the former pastors, whose tenures spanned three decades. Although many of the church's 260 current members were not the same men and women who caused the pastors to leave "wounded and deeply distressed," Joudry had congregants apologize for "misdeeds and un-Christlike attitudes," including gossip and publicly maligning them (11).

Jezebel's fate is recorded in II Kings 9:30-37. As with all demonic spirits, her fate was sealed. Even though it had been fourteen long years since Naboth was killed, God's justice wouldn't be denied. Ahab was killed (I Kings 22:37) and they washed the blood from his chariot where the prostitutes bathed and the dogs licked up his blood just as the Word of the Lord declared. Ahab's sons, Ahaziah and Joram, inherited their father's throne in turn and came to ignominious ends. In fact, Joram's dead body was thrown on the field which belonged to Naboth (II Kings 9:24-26).

Jehu was anointed king of Israel by Elisha, Elijah's successor (II Kings 9). He was commissioned to destroy the house of Ahab. He was given both the mission and permission to accomplish the task.

After Jehu killed Joram, he headed for Jezreel where

Jezebel "painted her eyes, arranged her hair and looked out of a window" (v. 30, NIV). Although some see this as an attempt at seduction, eye make-up was "antimony," eye paint found in early Egyptian graves. Jezebel knew her time had come. She was preparing to die.

"Have you come in peace, Zimri, you murderer of your master?" she asks (v. 31). Does the spirit of Jezebel ever want peace? She calls Jehu a traitor, but God is cleaning house! There was to be no treaty, no negotiations, and no compromise with Jezebel because there was no peaceful coexistence with her. She was unrepentant to the end.

Jehu echoes the words of Joshua as he looked up at Jezebel's window: "Who is on my side?" (v. 32). Jesus warned the church in Thyatira, "Nevertheless, I have this against you: you tolerate that woman Jezebel, who calls herself a prophetess. By her teaching she misleads my servants into sexual immorality and the eating of food sacrificed to idols. I have given her time to repent of her immorality, but she is unwilling. So I will cast her on a bed of suffering, and I will make those who commit adultery with her suffer intensely, unless they repent of her ways" (Revelation 2:20-22).

Jezebel was thrown from a high window and her blood spattered the wall of the palace. Horses trampled her underfoot (vv. 32-33). Jehu ordered her to be buried, but by the time they got to her body there was nothing left but her skull, her feet, and her hands (v. 35). All of this was in accordance with the word of the Lord spoken by Elijah. Any identification of her was destroyed. God wanted to make sure nothing remained for anyone to worship, recognize, or mourn.

Be on your guard for the Jezebel spirit in your church. Recognize the traits under which it operates. Wait until you have the permission of the Lord to address her sin. As God's instrument, you are an enemy of the Jezebel spirit, but more than a conqueror for without a hostage, Jezebel has no power. Therefore, encourage repentance with those who foster conflict. Repentance cleanses. Repentance brings the presence of Jesus.

CHAPTER 5

Expectations

"The odds of hitting a duffed shot increase by the square of the number of people watching" (Henry Beard, *Mulligan's Laws)*.

South Carolina Southern Baptists lead the nation in the number of suicides among active pastors. In the recent past, eight men in eight years ended their own lives. In addition, more South Carolina Baptist pastors and staff are fired annually than anywhere else in the nation. My friend, Dr. Jim Austin, the retired former executive director-treasurer of the South Carolina Baptist Convention said, "There's never been a time in modern American life where expectations for a pastor are so high and the appreciation extended to them is so low."

Even though a preacher is self-employed for tax purposes, he or she has as many bosses as there are members in a church. Any seasoned member of the clergy will tell you when he or she assumes the leadership in a new parish, you must learn the church history, culture, and their time-honored traditions. A minister must then balance what is expected with what is reasonable. Oftentimes, if a balance is not struck there's the real or perceived risk of jeopardizing one's employment. Dr. Herb Reavis, the pastor of North Jacksonville Baptist Church, wryly quipped, "People only like two pastors. The one they used to have and the one they're going to have." Much of this has to do with the extrinsic and intrinsic pressures unique to the ministry.

Extrinsic Pressures

In one church I served, the pastor with the longest tenure was legendary in his response to congregational needs. He drove long distances for hospital or home-bound visits, even traveling out-of-state. His status was so elevated I was told he even mowed the parsonage lawn in a suit! The difficulty comes when members refuse to let go of the gold standard set by an icon. If the new pastor doesn't measure up to the legend, the congregation may act more spoiled than a Beverly Hills housewife.

A pastor is subject to the unusual requests well-meaning people make. "Preacher, will you go see my wife's aunt's brother-in-law's second cousin's friend? He's in the hospital and doesn't have a home church. He doesn't have a pastor. I know you're busy, but if you get a chance could you visit him, *please*?" Another may suggest, "My neighbor died and her family doesn't attend church. I know you don't know her or her family, but would you mind doing her funeral?"

There are those who expect the minister to make

financial sacrifices. In one church I pastored, I met with our treasurer and other leaders about the possibility of giving me a travel allowance. The treasurer traveled the world in the IT profession and was reimbursed for all his travel. However, he was the point man for not giving me the allowance. What was his rationale? "It's not my fault you chose the ministry." The only thing more shocking than the look on my face was the fact a lightning bolt didn't pierce the roof and sear him to a cinder.

Pastors are expected to maintain a certain image. I once had a member drive by my house when I was working in the yard on a hot summer day. To my detriment, I wasn't wearing a suit. He mentioned I was shirtless while weeding my bushes. Someone else sarcastically commented on black socks I wore when mowing my yard. One Sunday morning, we had our Vacation Bible School celebration and a member was offended because I wore shorts.

In addition, ministers are expected to be "on" at any given time whether shopping at a Walmart or present at an event. One particularly demanding Saturday, I conducted a funeral in the morning. I did my best to minister to the grieving family. In the afternoon, I officiated at a large outdoor wedding. Flipping such an emotional switch can be difficult.

Abe, Donna, Evan, Frank, Gwen, and Hank all struggled with extrinsic pressures. They chose their profession because they wished to aid people. Like a low-flying goose sucked into the engine of a plane, though, they were caught in the vortex of trying to please people. Pastors are victimized by extrinsic pressures when they engage in behavior to earn rewards or avoid punishment.

Intrinsic Pressures

Intrinsic motivation for clergy starts with a divine call. Every participant in this study described a specific time or unusual event connected to God's call on his or her life. You can't perform in the ministry without a clear and definitive call from God. Think of those who ran from God's call like me. My conscience bothered me. I constantly struggled internally to reconcile the negative things happening in my life against the "might have beens" if I had obeyed the Lord. Once I repented and answered my call to ministry, I was ONLY able to endure the extrinsic pressures because of the internal resolve God provided as I sought to fulfill His purpose.

Self-imposed stress results from a failure to meet one's own benchmarks. What pastor doesn't want to be on the speaking circuit? What minister wouldn't love to stand before large crowds on Sunday mornings? What preacher wouldn't like to have a stack of books in print like "Ten Steps to Humility and

How I Made it in Nine." What cleric wouldn't like to retire at a reasonable age like his peers in other professions? Interestingly, only one of the respondents in my study indicated finances as a source of stress. Media-types may sarcastically skewer preachers they believe "holla for a dolla," but these dedicated men and women aren't in it for the money.

Preachers are vulnerable to the same siren songs of competition and comparison. If we aren't careful, intrinsic pressures can be fatal to our reputation and well-being.

Expectation Examples

Abe attended conferences and conventions where, inevitably, the question was asked, "How big is your church?" He ruefully noted, "That's the first question someone asks!" He was exasperated, "They can't see faithfulness and they can't see all the nights you spend in the hospital and they can't see all the time you put in with the children of the church."

Donna was criticized by one member for taking vacation around the holidays, re-enforcing his complaint with "people weren't pleased." She explained, "He always says, 'people,' but he will never identify who the people are. I'm always here." During graduation season she was expected to attend all the students' open houses.

Evan offered, "There are always people wanting you to do things." He cited the cooperative effort of several churches in his community for Vacation Bible School. "I'm doing nothing with Vacation Bible School other than promoting it." Then he received a letter from the committee in charge: "We're encouraging the pastors of supporting churches to be present at the school Monday, Tuesday, Wednesday, Thursday, and Friday evening." He smirked, "Okay, I don't really have to do anything. They just want me there from six to nine on Monday, Tuesday, Wednesday, Thursday, Friday unless of course I can't come." With a modicum of sarcasm he intoned, "But if I can't come, I certainly can't be sitting in the backyard. That's the expectations people have." His therapist diagnosed him with "compassion fatigue."

Frank recalled an incident with the Mutual Ministry Committee and did a low boil, "They wanted me fired because at two o'clock in the afternoon I was dressed in my clerical collar, pushing my son in a stroller when I should have been working even though it was my lunch hour. Of course, they didn't bother to ask that." Frank's hot seat moment was fueled by one individual. "This person, of course, was someone that can't be happy with life, wasn't happy with their own life, not happy with anything." Thankfully, this wildfire was readily extinguished by the appropriate people.

As a female in ministry, Gwen faced role expectations related to her gender. Her New Testament seminary professor "was overtly against women in ministry." She felt this same lack of affirmation in her church. Early in her seminary studies when she thought she might pursue a career as a counselor, she received a great deal of support: "The people at the church we were attending said, 'Bravo! Bravo! That's great!'" However, when she decided to switch vocations and become a pastor, the vocal cheer-leading by her colleagues diminished dramatically. "The response was much cooler, much more distant. That was probably the first deep pain I felt in being ostracized or disapproved by people I thought really cared about me."

Hank switched from a career in insurance to one in ministry and the expectations were strikingly different. "As an insurance agent you could separate. You had your work hours whether they were ten hours a day or twelve hours a day or six hours a day. [As an insurance agent] I would go to church, go to the ball field and not deal with insurance-related issues." The ramifications for a pastor were much different. "Here, this is all you are. This is your work. This is your church. These are your friends. There's no separation. There's no release." He doesn't engage in activities such as golf. "I don't feel like I have the time to do those things." Hank grew a bit morose, "A day off just meant I wasn't in the office. I was doing ministry somewhere else." It's relentless, "I can be sitting there watching TV and I don't have a clue what's going on TV and my mind is going a million miles an hour. I'm just figuring out the next stage."

Expectations are like weeds in a paved parking lot. You think they're covered and they emerge from a crack. The responsibilities for a pastor include hospital ministry, counseling, sermon preparation, leadership of staff, vision-casting for volunteers, grief intervention, home visitation, and attendance at both church and extra-church functions. Only three participants took a regular day off which reveals the expectations and the time pressures a pastor faces.

Nearly all my participants mentioned they are rarely clear of their obligations. Role ambiguity, role overload, and not knowing what's expected contribute to stress for professionals (1). Siburt and Wray (2) confirmed ministers believe they must do all things well and must always be available.

The studies revealed by Lee and Iverson-Gilbert (3) involved unrealistic and intrusive expectations pressed on clergy by their congregations. The more demanding the congregation, the lower the pastor's well-being and life satisfaction, and the higher his or her burnout. The literature revealed expectations, time demands, and role overload were all culprits when a pastor became overwhelmed (4).

Donna felt pressure to be always available and had trouble saying, "No." Hank pointed to his head and confessed, "This never shuts down." Hank also admitted his biggest issue was "not knowing how to say, 'No.'" All the demands led to his depression and he even contemplated suicide. Evan was so intent upon satisfying the expectations of others he found himself stale, lacking energy and creativity. He conceded about a year and a half earlier he was getting tired, inefficient, not functioning well "and I'm not sure what to do." He admitted, "Sometimes, I don't care."

Think of the incredible demands placed upon Elijah as God's prophet. After praying intensely, it wouldn't rain in Israel, God answered his prayer and God called upon Elijah to give King Ahab the news in person (I Kings 17:1). Next, God sent him to the Kerith Ravine where he waited in obscurity while the drought took effect. He subsisted on water from the brook and food brought to him by ravens (I Kings 17:5-6). When the nation-wide drought caused his water source to run dry, God told him to move to Zarephath (I Kings 17:9). There, against Jewish custom, he relied on a poverty-stricken widow to supply a roof over his head and food for his stomach. While living in Zarephath atop Ahab's "Most Wanted List," the widow's son died and Elijah prayed God would allow the boy's life to return to him (I Kings 17:21) and God answered his prayer.

In I Kings 18, God instructed Elijah to present himself a second time to Ahab because Yahweh was about to send rain upon the land. As Elijah made the long trek back across the desert and countryside from Sidon to Israel, he saw the severe effects in Samaria (I Kings 18:2). Not only were the riverbeds cracked and empty but only dry roots were evidence of once green grass. The trees were barren and skeletal remains of starved animals littered the fields. Do you think Elijah had second thoughts about his prayer for revival as he viewed these different scenes on his journey? Do you think he dreaded another meeting with his adversary, the potentate of Israel? Queen Jezebel was killing the Lord's prophets (verse 4). The prospect of adding Elijah's head to her trophy collection of martyrs fueled the evil queen's vendetta.

Contrast Elijah's predicament with the privileges enjoyed by Obadiah, the governor of Ahab's palace (I Kings 18:3). Obadiah was "a devout believer of the Lord" (v. 3). How he was able to finagle this position with Ahab and Jezebel remains a mystery. How could a devout believer serve with such ungodly people? Verse four indicates Obadiah hid 100 of the Lord's prophets in two different caves and supplied them with food and water. His act was commendable given the adversarial climate in Israel against the Lord's anointed. Obadiah knew how to play whatever political games necessary in order to survive. It's not beyond reason to expect God made it possible for Obadiah to serve in such a capacity. God has been known to place people in difficult circumstances to accomplish His purposes. If God can have Joseph sold as a slave, the baby Moses placed in a basket of reeds, Daniel thrown to the lions, and Esther win a beauty contest, then God can certainly use Obadiah in an idolatrous palace. God has also placed you where you are for a reason and a season. He's locked in to your GPS signal. Your friends or foes may think they can control your time, but only God controls your future.

In his classic treatise, *The Making of a Leader*, Dr. J. Robert Clinton (5) discusses the importance of an inner-life process known as "integrity checks." God will use four areas to prove a leader's mettle.

First, values determine convictions. The word "ethics" is derived from the Greek word "ethos," which means a stall, a hiding place. Think of this as a place where a person goes to find security, an immovable refuge. The word "morals," on the other hand, is derived from the word "mores" which means "always changing." The temperature of moral culture has changed dramatically from ten, twenty, even fifty years ago. Society's morals may change more than a fifteen-year-old girl's hairstyles, but individual values which determine convictions should be a refuge for a leader. Alexander Solzhenitsyn wrote, "The line between good and evil does not pass between principalities and powers, but it oscillates within the human heart."

Second, temptation tests convictions. One couple decided to visit a fine eatery one night, but failed to make reservations. When they arrived, several people were signed up for a table ahead of them. The husband left his name with the hostess and waited. Within earshot, the husband overheard a disgruntled couple leave the restaurant, complaining the wait was too long. Within minutes, the hostess called, "Walker? Walker?" No one responded. She called again, "Walker?" but her query went unanswered. Quickly, the husband convinced his wife if he told the hostess they were the Walkers, they could be seated faster. The wife succumbed to her husband's duplicitous plea. As the couple approached the hostess, she asked, "Walker?" The husband nodded. "We've been expecting you," she informed the conspiratorial couple. "Your family is waiting in the dining room."

Third, persecution tests steadfastness. When persecution comes, the Apostle Paul reminds us, "Whatever you do, work at it with all your heart, as working for the Lord, not for men, since you know that you will receive an inheritance from the Lord as a reward. It is the Lord Christ you are serving" (Colossians

3:23-24). We answer to an audience of One, Almighty God. World War II General, George S. Patton, once came across some of his officers who appeared more concerned for their own personal safety than they were about leading their men forward. General Patton shouted, "Do you want to give your men the idea that the enemy is dangerous?!" The place of God's calling is the place of God's keeping.

Fourth, loyalty tests allegiance. In ancient Greece, the politically crafty philosopher Aristippus learned to get along in court by flattering the tyrant, Denys. Aristippus looked down his nose at some of his less prosperous fellow philosophers and wise men who wouldn't stoop so low. One day, Aristippus saw his colleague Diogenes washing some vegetables and he said to him disdainfully, "If you would only learn to flatter King Denys you would not have to be washing lentils." Diogenes looked up slowly and in the same tone replied, "And you, if you had only learned to live on lentils, would not have to flatter King Denys." D. L. Moody is credited with saying, "If I am to walk alone, let me walk alone with God."

So, how do you discern between fulfilling God's call on your life and the cacophony of expectations from your parishioners? If you constantly spend your time trying to accomplish the latter, in all likelihood you will never accomplish the former.

Carmen Berry, a social worker, fell victim to the tyranny of expectations. She generally devoted six days a week to her profession, volunteered at her church, served on committees, and saw clients before the Sunday morning and evening services. As a result, she was exhausted and her relationships were unsatisfying. In 1984, physically sick and emotionally spent, she took a year off, quit her job and no longer attended church. She began a spiritual journey of prayer and therapy. She admitted the year with God was the basis of her recovery.

From her experience and work with numerous driven clients emerged Berry's concept of the "Messiah Trap." In her book, *When Helping You is Hurting Me: Escaping the Messiah Trap* (6), she explained "Messiahs" are so busy taking care of others they don't take care of themselves. How do you fall victim to the "Messiah Trap"? When you neglect yourself because you feel you're supposed to sacrifice your own well-being for the sake of others. Berry explained Jesus illustrated in a balanced fashion how to minister. He took time to pray. He took time for personal relationships. He didn't respond to every need and He knew when to say, "No."

Bronnie Ware (7) spent years caring for patients in their last days. She identified the five most common regrets the dying expressed about how they lived their lives. The number one regret expressed was "I wish I'd had the courage to live a life true to myself, not the life others expected of me." Number 2: "I wish I hadn't worked so hard." Number 3: "I wish I'd had the courage to express my feelings." Number 4: "I wish I'd stayed in touch with my friends." Number 5: "I wish that I had let myself be happier."

Samuel Chand (8) offers four strategies to manage the unrealistic expectations placed on pastors. First, focus on what you can control. Your scope of responsibility and power are limited. Devote your energies to those things inside your sandbox. You can't control the universe including your church environment. Mark Owen (9) described a great tactic for controlling what you can control. His Navy SEAL group trained for scaling mountains. Positioned in the Nevada desert, Owen was assigned a partner to lead him to the summit. Owen confessed his inherent fear of heights took a toll. As he scaled the sheer face of the mountain he was using more cams and pitons than necessary and wasn't going to have enough to reach the summit. Complicating this was his glances down at his partner below as well as the desert floor. He would also steal glimpses at the glitter of Las Vegas. In short, he froze and he wouldn't move any further. Just then, one of the civilian instructors aiding the candidates sliced his way to Owen's side. The civilian was nothing like a Navy SEAL, but swung across the face of the mountain like Spiderman. He knew Owen was in trouble and asked him why. Owen admitted he was distracted and this caused his fears to well up in him and halt his progress. To which the civilian climbing expert replied, "You need to focus on your three-foot world. Looking at Las Vegas or the summit or down at the desert is not helping you. Focus on the three feet in front of you. Focus on what you can control and you will make it." Owen took his advice and scaled the rest of the mountain without incident.

The second strategy suggested by Chand is to be tenaciously thankful. Exchange your griping for gratitude. Despite the unreasonable demands and long hours of your work in the church, is there something for which you can be grateful every day? If the Apostle Paul could be chained to a Praetorian Guard in a Roman prison cell awaiting execution and still write the Epistle of Joy known as Philippians, can you could find something to smile about today?

Third, resolve any alignment issues. When the job description doesn't fit a person's gifts and interests, confusion and heartache inevitably occur (p. 92). Mission fit and church culture may contribute to lack of alignment. Chand suggests, you may not have a perfect fit, but a "good enough fit" could make it easier for the individual, team and mission to work well together. Take a clue from David when King Saul called him to his tent. Goliath the giant was frothing at the mouth. David volunteered to engage the Philistine in battle. When King Saul unbelievably accepted young David's courageous offer, he promptly tried to put his own expectations on David by making him wear his armor. David politely indulged his king, but graciously deflected his request. He was more comfortable going into battle with his tools. All the time in the pasture paid dividends and we should follow David's lead. Know who you are. Accept who you are. Be who you are.

Finally, invest creative capital: "In stagnant, discouraging, and toxic cultures, people spend their energies protecting themselves and creating alliances instead of creatively pursuing the mission" (p. 92). Deep disappointments can be caused by unrealistic expectations and shattered dreams. Take the time to address these challenges with courage and hope. Invest yourself in the cause which drew you in the first place.

CHAPTER 6

Crises

"Accept that some days you're the pigeon, and some days
you're the statue" (Roger C. Andersen, *The Rotarian).*

King Ahab sat idly by as his pagan queen mercilessly executed
God's prophets. She desired the same for Elijah. Despite this
imminent danger, the courageous prophet sent for Ahab (I Kings
18). The king of Israel appeared and hypocritically denounced
God's man as the "troubler of Israel" (v. 17). How many pastors
are characterized as troublemakers by antagonistic members? "'I
have not made trouble for Israel,' Elijah replied. 'But you and
your father's family have. You have abandoned the Lord's
commands and have followed the Baals'" (v. 18). It was time for
a showdown of truth versus error, righteousness against evil,
God's way over man's way.

Elijah instructed Israel's king to summon the people to
Mt. Carmel and bring the 450 prophets of Baal and 400 prophets
of Asherah. Mt. Carmel, part of a mountain ridge fifteen miles
long and 470 feet high at the point selected by Elijah, was a
perfect location for the prophet to confront Jezebel's minions.
Carmel means "fruitful garden" and possessed lush vegetation.
Today, it's known for beautiful orchids. The Carmel ridge

served as a border between Israel and the Phoenicians from whom Baal worship originated. Asherah was known as the "earth-mother." Baal was the god of fertility, the god of the storm, present in the dew and the rain. Elijah wasn't waiting for a spine donor. He would've echoed a statement by Holocaust survivor, Corrie Ten Boom, centuries later, "God has plans, not problems, for our lives."

Tichy & Bennis (1) believe good leaders anticipate crises. Further, they "prepare themselves and their organizations to respond effectively and efficiently when they do" (p. 210). The vast majority of people base their opinion of their preacher just on Sunday. The Navy SEAL motto, "The only easy day was yesterday" (2) could easily apply to the ministry. Many never see a pastor as a first responder to a family in crisis at 1:00 A.M. or receiving an emergency call on a day off. As in any profession, a leader must have the capability not only to personally cope with the ripple effects of such circumstances, but have the capacity to help others navigate the situation successfully. The ability to be adept at both may determine a lengthy or truncated pastorate.

The Crisis of a Lost Call

The search committee neglected to mention the multiple splits prior to Abe's arrival. "When we moved here I felt like I stepped into a hornet's nest." Members had been fighting for many years. By his estimate, three or four pastors were forced to leave. As the church began to grow under Abe's leadership, an "older group" resisted any attempts to assimilate new people. Abe admitted the church began to split "and I could actually see it happening. About thirty-five people left, but they were the ones with all the money." This pathological behavior employed with previous pastors was a manipulation technique. Abe stated, "They knew how to work the system."

A veteran of twenty-four years in the ministry, Abe soon found himself without a place to preach when his church was closed by the district leaders. This happened after the District Superintendent promised Abe would be involved in the decision, but "he just did it without me." The district closed the church because "they just got tired of messing with this group of people."

When the church was closed, Abe lost his job, his only source of income, and his family had no money. Devastated, Abe had no interest in pursuing another church, "I really was just worn out." When I spoke with him, he was selling insurance instead of engaged in ministry. "I feel guilty because I almost feel dead inside; I mean, as far as *the call*. Used to be I was so clear about everything. I knew exactly what I was going to do...and since this happened, man, I don't know what to do. I don't know what to tell anybody looking for direction in their lives. I'm looking for the passion I used to have for ministry... I feel like I'm fighting an 800-pound gorilla. I could tell you all the Scriptures, but I'm not sure it works. It hasn't been working for me lately. My biggest problem now is just lack of direction, lack of focus, lack of passion...I feel like it's been burned out." His voice grew very quiet. "I felt since I was 12, I knew what ...I was gonna do, but I don't know anymore."

The Crisis of Personal Attacks

Of Ben's thirty-two years in ministry, twenty-five were invested in his present church. Before his sixth year was completed, nine members conspired to fire Ben. They maneuvered to force a termination vote during a Sunday morning worship service. Ben confidently reminisced, "they couldn't do it because the people, the spirit of the people and the spirit of the worship service" overpowered their negative intent. Later, the mutineers recruited sixty people at a Monday night meeting and created nearly three pages of grievances against their pastor. Six weeks later, the conspirators were able to finagle a four-hour congregational meeting. Ben was accused of "misappropriation of funds" which was an elaborate fabrication. Ben emphasized the schemers were the church check-signers and was amazed at how "mean-spirited people can be," but he was prepared. A stickler for details, Ben had every financial record from his tenure placed on the offering table for anyone's perusal. Ben chimed, "Well, guess what? They said all the things they wanted to say and we dismissed the meeting and I was still the pastor!" Ben made a decision not to meet with the toxic members anymore, "and by the power of prayer, every one of them left our church."

The Crisis of Accidents

Within months of Chet's appointment, tragedy struck. His newly-hired youth pastor was supervising a mission project in the local community. The youth pastor's wife drove their sixteen-month-old son to the site for a visit. As she was making the turn onto the property, a delivery truck rear-ended her vehicle. Her car burst into flames. The youth pastor, along with nearly two-dozen church people working on the property, witnessed the catastrophe. The youth pastor scrambled to pull his wife from the burning wreckage and suffered severe burns. His wife was in a coma for three months with forty percent of her upper body burned. The baby died. Chet returned home late the night of the accident and his nine-year old daughter kept asking how he was doing. Chet softly intoned, "We held each other for a while. That was the first time she'd seen me in the level of stress...I don't know if she'd ever seen me cry."

A week later, Chet was attending an ordination class in a neighboring state when he was notified a ten-year-old boy in the congregation hanged himself. The little guy was in the hospital and "it didn't look good," mourned Chet. "I just about lost my mind completely that day...it was the stress. At that moment, I was wondering, if this kid dies, how in the world am I gonna deal with this and how are we gonna survive it?"

The boy did survive, but while Chet was preparing for his return trip from the ordination class, he received even more bad news. Another staff member called to let him know of an anonymous letter criticizing the worship leader. Chet indicated something took place internally on his return trip. "The stress of the accident, the stress of this new issue, and the sudden emergence of a non-issue ...caused me to make an unconscious intentional decision I would do whatever it took to protect my congregation and my staff over the next two months with whatever was going to take place."

In the six months after the automobile accident "I had to walk people through the grieving process." The life of the youth pastor's wife hung in the balance. "We still didn't know if she was going to survive." Further complicating matters, the company for which the truck driver worked was a respected and long-time fixture in the community. The young truck driver was well-known and well-regarded in the church and the town. This conflagration of stressful demands was overwhelming for a first-year lead pastor.

Members of the church were divided over what actions, if any, the youth minister should take in response to the driver who caused the accident. It all grew to be too much. Chet confided, "A combination of things finally came to a head. There was finally a moment when I knew I couldn't carry it any longer." The church board graciously granted Chet and his family a three-week sabbatical. It did wonders for his psyche, but upon his return, his secretary greeted him: "There's a newspaper article on the lawsuit" the youth pastor had filed. Chet sighed, "Within an hour, I had a phone call from one of my 'thorns.'" Chet came to a conclusion: "By Wednesday I came home and said, 'I can't do this. I just cannot.' I didn't have the emotional capacity."

The Crisis of Self Doubt

Like a combination punch from a boxer, Donna was reeling from the stress: "We are having so many people in crises in their personal lives. I mean I've had three marriages in the eleven years I've been here that ended in divorce. A young man had been in jail and you try to counsel with the family who's torn apart." Her voice grew quieter when she indicated it "has been very stressful when you see people you love and their lives are just falling apart." One couple in the church didn't want anyone to know they were undergoing marriage counseling. They asked Donna to attend the weekly sessions with them in a neighboring town. She said, "This lasted six months. You fall in love with these people and then you see they are hurting so bad…their marriage ends in divorce. That's just real hard for me to watch. You start second-guessing yourself. My major in [college] was psychology, but there's some things I just don't feel like I'm equipped to handle."

The Crisis of Arson

Frank's former church was the target of an arsonist. Even though Frank was in a new parish when he related this sad story, the experience left emotional scars from nine years earlier. "It was a beautiful church," he sighed. The building dated to 1906 with an educational wing added in 1962. Investigators concluded the arsonist ignited the fire on Frank's office desk.

"I lost everything. Stuff the kids made, stuff my wife

made, stuff people made. Ninety-nine-point five percent of my library basically was incinerated." It was hard for him to grasp the totality of the loss: the un-apprehended arsonist, the loss of the facilities, and the event itself. "If you catch me at certain moments, it's still hard to talk about. It's something how you tie your faith to a facility. I saw grown men cry I would have bet a million dollars I never would have seen shed a tear even at their own mother's funeral. Seeing the fire move throughout the building; it was just devastating for everybody."

A few months earlier, the congregation had roofed the sanctuary with fifty-year shingles. "The roof caved in," he sighed deeply. The firemen were positioned on a wooden wheelchair ramp. "One of the firemen yelled, 'Get out of there!' and the roof kind of came to the center and then bowed out the walls and so all the brick fell on (long pause) three guys." All of them were flown by life-flight to a nearby hospital "and they were fine because the wooden wheelchair ramp gave way. It gave them a cushion. It's hard to describe. In a way you visualize it and in a way it's kind of blanked out. Hearing them [the firefighters] yelling and screaming and getting them out of there, you know, was bad... really bad."

Due to the extensive damage, the architect recommended razing the structure. Frank stated, "I wanted to crawl under a rock and hide." The congregation "experienced a death," he said. "It was intentional rather than accidental, salt in an open wound, and seeing the building standing there was like seeing a dead person. Then I had to lead them through the burial which is when we razed the building."

Frank had to deal with his own emotions, "I was royally ticked off and that's putting it mildly at whoever did this. There was no resolution – no closure." Through the process he grew angry with some of the members of the congregation, "The troublemakers all saw this as a good opportunity to raise trouble in the midst of a troubling situation."

The Crisis of an Estranged Child

Gwen's son was romantically involved with the daughter of an influential family in her church. The influential family constantly spoke negatively about his parents while he was away at college. "His girlfriend was in a storm cloud," explained Gwen. Her son asked his girlfriend what was wrong and she spewed, "I hate your parents." There was a catch in Gwen's voice as she recalled this painful memory. When the youth pastor resigned, the influential family, supporters of the youth pastor and antagonists of Gwen, exited the church as well. As a result, Gwen's son wanted to attend church with his girlfriend's family. To keep the peace, Gwen and her husband conceded he could attend the other church one Sunday a month, but it soon grew to be more. Eventually, Gwen's son ran away from home, "We didn't know where he was."

Gwen and her husband solicited their congregation's prayers for the return of their estranged son. Surprisingly, while they were on queue at a funeral home waiting to pay their respects, they discovered the whereabouts of their son. Unbeknownst to Gwen, he was staying with a prominent board member from her church! Simultaneously, Gwen and her husband discovered people in the church were also aware of their son's location. It was humiliating to realize all the time their son was missing and they requested prayer for his safe return, the congregants chose to keep his whereabouts a secret.

She sighed, "Talk about betrayal." For three years they tried to reconcile with their prodigal. Eventually, he married the influential family's daughter. "We didn't know where the wedding was until we got the invitation." She and her husband were neither included in the wedding plans nor the ceremony. Following her son's wedding, the church board gave Gwen a negative vote and her call to the church was not renewed. She was left without a church appointment. She mused, "Probably the first eighteen months, I didn't like to even think about people." Once she was ready, though, ministry opportunities were scarce. Open pulpits for female ministers who were forced

---

from office were in short supply.

Compounding all these events, she admitted to dealing with fibromyalgia." So, in addition to the normal stressors a person would have in the pastorate, there was this underlying physical disability." Fibromyalgia is a chronic condition with pain in the muscles and ligaments. Fatigue is also a common symptom. Gwen concluded, "What I struggle with is: was this God's design and purpose for [her husband] and me to go through all of this?" She began to weep as she characterized why God allowed these events. "This is My will for your life. You need some chastising. You need some humiliation, but then I would say, 'I'm cool with that.'"

The Crisis of Suicidal Thoughts

As a successful insurance agent, Hank was used to long days and hard work accompanied by material rewards. As a pastor, the long days and hard work never seemed to end. Answering God's call to become a pastor, the strategies he used to grow his business were the very things which helped him succeed as a pastor. "We haven't had any bad things happen here. I'm learning you can overdo a good thing. There are no cutoff hours in ministry. There is always a crisis and I love doin' it. I love being here. I love being the problem-fixer. Not knowing how to say, 'No,' those are probably things I'm wrestling with right now." He characterized the demands as the same as filling a cup. "You take that thing and you fill it up and there's just been constant stuff being put in there and at some point when it gets to the top, it doesn't take a whole lot to kick it over. I am battling extreme anxiety and depression." He traveled two and a half hours to see a therapist because he didn't want anyone in his congregation to know.

He sought professional help when he "decided to check out." I asked if he meant resigning from his church. Hank gazed intently at me, "I mean check out of life. I found myself sitting in the dark for three hours, staring out the window, totally dumb and decided I was done." His wife and kids returned home to find him sitting despondently in a dark room with a loaded gun in his hands. When he visited a medical doctor he was asked, "Have you ever thought about killing yourself?" Hank said, "I just paused. I'm a pastor of a successful church. I have all the answers. How do I answer?" The doctor diagnosed him as "highly depressed" and prescribed medications didn't work initially. Hank was then referred to a psychiatrist who adjusted his medications.

Hank felt his extremely rough childhood had a latent effect on his adult condition, "At eleven years old I had to grow up." He paused thoughtfully. He didn't go into detail about his family except their lives included, "Livin' mean, jail, and drugs." He was haunted constantly by the sins of his family of origin, "I had a fear of turning out like that…scared to death."

Just months prior to our interview, Hank attended a conference and heard a fellow pastor recount "a crash in his life." It was Hank's epiphany, "For the first time, I heard a speaker begin to describe what I'd been experiencing. I'd been afraid to say anything about it to anyone because I didn't think anyone would understand. I began to bawl like a baby. I lost it… because somebody finally got what I was going through."

He characterized the irony of his situation, "I mean I was running like crazy. I don't burn out. Everybody else burns out, but I don't burn out. And to see me here, right now and to hear the things coming out of my mouth – it would never happen to me." No one in his church knew about his condition except his staff. "Nobody here has a clue." At the same time, he admitted he needs the compassion of his congregation, "Or I'm probably not going to be able to make it much longer."

He described himself as being "authentic," but he wasn't quite comfortable sharing his ordeal with his congregation. "This is the one issue I haven't felt I'm prepared to get out there all the way." Hank's not afraid to tell his people, "I'm messing up." He anticipated some type of collateral effects, perhaps emotional or professional, and he confessed, "I'm just not ready to deal with it yet."

Considering the responses above, it's important to note how each one processed acute stress induced by a crisis. By the nature of their profession, pastors often live from crisis to crisis since they're often the first ones called by their flock. Regular runs to hospitals, mortuaries, or to a home where a family is in dire need of comfort, creates an enormous demand on a preacher. The unknown requires clergy to be ready psychologically, emotionally, physically, and spiritually to handle any situation with calm, tact, and aplomb. A U. S. military officer in Afghanistan once noted, "Most people flee at the sound of gunfire. Soldiers run toward it." The same is true for clergy as they respond to a variety of crises in the parish.

People often ignore how a minister handles personal emotions as a result of the event. Whether clergy are directly or indirectly affected by a crisis may determine their ability to moderate the stress. If crises are concurrent, it may lead to acute stress, which in turn could produce stress-induced analgesia (3).* The pastor will continue to operate in a world driven by chaos with the potential for disastrous personal results.

"Elijah went before the people and said, 'How long will you waver between two opinions? If the Lord is God, follow Him; but if Baal is God, follow him" (v. 21). The people said nothing. The onlookers were there only by command of wicked

King Ahab. The Israelites could care less. They just wanted to see who would put on the best show. They were looking for any kind of amusement to pass another boring drought day. The wheel was turning, but the hamster was dead.

Elijah challenged the 450 prophets of Baal, but the 400 prophets of Asherah were nowhere to be found. Maybe Jezebel hid them. Maybe they were just afraid of the man of God. The prophets of Baal must have been jazzed with the conditions because Elijah gave them every advantage. They were given first choice of one of the two bulls available for sacrifice, "Then you call on the name of your god, and I will call on the name of the LORD. The god who answers by fire – he is God" (vv. 23-24). Don't you love Elijah's optimism in the midst of a crisis? He used the traditional Hebrew name, *Elohim,* which indicates Jehovah as the Creator and Judge of the universe (Genesis 1:1-2:4a). Elijah's God would answer by fire even though the pagan god, Baal, was the supposed sun god, the "controller of nature."

The Baal prophets exhausted themselves from morning until noon. They prostrated themselves before their altar. They pleaded and cried to Baal, their god of thunderstorms, hail, rain, and lightning. Imagine the scene: flies collecting on the bullock's carcass as it bloats in the mid-day heat, vultures and ravens circling overhead waiting to dive on an easy meal. Meanwhile, the sky is as blue as Tanzanite. "At noon, Elijah began to taunt them, 'Shout louder!' he said. 'Surely he is a god! Perhaps he is deep in thought, or busy, or traveling. Maybe he is sleeping and must be awakened'" (v.27). "So they shouted louder and slashed themselves with swords and spears, as was their custom, until the blood flowed" (v. 28). "Midday passed, and they continued their frantic prophesying until the time for the evening sacrifice. But there was no response, no one answered, no one paid attention" (v. 29).

Elijah provides sage insight on how to respond in a crisis. Even though one may never truly be prepared for a traumatic event, Elijah took the battle to the enemy. By preparing the altar first, he focused on worship, not the crisis. He carefully stacked twelve stones in three rows of four. God's law stated, "The fire shall ever be burning upon the altar; it shall never go out" (Leviticus 6:13). The fire of Israel's religious fervor had long been extinguished. If you're in the midst of your own crisis, ask yourself two questions. First, are you living on yesterday's ashes? Second, are you worshipping at a broken altar?

Elijah built a trench around the altar to hold water, the hide of the bullock, the entrails, dung and residue. The trench separated the altar as holy ground. The altar of the Baalist prophets represented the profane, the common in Israel. God's servant needs to know there's a place of refuge set apart for worship and focus on a holy God, my Rock in the midst of a crisis.

Plenty of dead trees littered the landscape after a three-and-a-half-year drought. It also symbolized Israel's idol worship. Elijah gathered the dead wood and placed it on the sacrifice; an act of anticipation God would supernaturally provide what the prophet needed.

Elijah then meticulously prepared the bull. He bled it carefully, quartered and jointed it. There was significance behind Elijah's demand a bullock be used. He didn't request a lamb, a bushel of grain or a pair of doves. He wanted an ox. A priest, a prophet, a man of God offered an ox in sacrifice to God only for his own private sins. Elijah was declaring his own unworthiness! He modeled a humility which required cleansing and purification as God's servant. The bull was a sin offering. God draws near to the one who senses his own sin and seeks cleansing. This doesn't imply a crisis is always the evidence of sin, but it serves us well to examine our own hearts so we aren't guilty of sin in dealing with the crisis.

The prophet then had the people participate. "'Fill four large jars with water and pour it on the offering and on the wood. Do it again,' he said, and they did it again. 'Do it a third time,' he ordered, and they did it the third time. The water soaked the carcass and ran down the sides of the altar in rivulets, completely filling the trench."

Two questions arise from this act. First, why did Elijah involve the people? They needed to be involved in the sacrifice and take responsibility for the condition the country faced. They were enacting a gesture they too had sinned. Second, where did they get the water? It would've been retrieved from the Mediterranean Sea, a distance below the site. As a result, they would've poured salt water on the altar. Salt was essential in every sacrifice. There would be no flies around the altar of Yahweh. The salt water repelled the flies. Salt was also a symbol of friendship and fidelity. The Israelites were ready to restore their relationship with God. Salt was the universal medication for healing wounds. I like Ron Hutchcraft's description, "Elijah got things ready for a fire only God could send. He acted like fire would come; doing everything he could do, trusting God to do what only He could do."

By then, it was late in the day. The orange glow of the setting sun casts the scene in an eerie light. This was the time of sacrifice. "Elijah stepped forward and prayed, 'O LORD, God of Abraham, Isaac, and Israel, let it be known today that you are God in Israel and that I am your servant and have done all these things at your command'" (v. 36). Despite the circumstances or the overwhelming odds or the incredible emotional toll from a crisis, God can still let it be known He is in control. As faithful ministers, if we know we've done everything in our power we can do, then surely, we can echo the words of Elijah, "I am your servant." Elijah was right with God as proven by his faithfulness in the Kerith ravine. He was right with others because he didn't discriminate against the widow of Zarephath. He knew he was in God's place in God's time even though Ahab and the prophets of Baal were staring daggers in his back. Elijah unflinchingly cried out, "Answer me, O LORD, answer me, so these people will know that you, O LORD, are God, and that you are turning their hearts back again" (v. 37).

Suddenly, a ball of flame fell like a comet on Elijah's sacrifice. The fire completely consumed the soggy sacrifice, the wet wood, the slathered stones, the soaked soil and even the saltwater sitting in the rock-hard trench. In a nano-second, the entire monument was oxidized! Only a black, smoldering hole in the ground remained. The spectators cried, "The LORD – he is God! The LORD – he is God!" (v. 39). Everyone's face was flush on the ground in humility before the majesty of Almighty God. The only one not prostrate was Elijah. He immediately called for the people to slaughter the prophets of Baal. They had to get rid of every vestige of sin and promptly obeyed God's man.

Surviving a crisis starts with my own spiritual condition. As you reflect on what you're experiencing, are you living on yesterday's ashes? Do you need to confess any sin of your own like Elijah? Once you do then you can get things ready for a fire only God can send.

* See Chapter 10 for a discussion of this condition.

CHAPTER 7

Loneliness

"There are 50 boys here at camp. I wish there were 49"

(An eleven-year-old's note home to his parents).

Have you ever had a glorious Elijah moment where all your hard work and faith finally made it feel like the fire fell from heaven? God honored your fasting and intercession and someone was healed. You stuck to your principles and you were vindicated. You studied and prepared and preached with such anointing people flooded the altar. Your mission trip was your best ever. You accomplished all your objectives and one of your team members answered the call to be a missionary…and then you crashed.

The internal demands you place on yourself cause stress as you seek to achieve. You strive to be a success in your own eyes and in the eyes of your spouse and your children. In the back of your head, a little voice reminds you of your high school or college reunion fast approaching and you better not attend if you don't have some kind of achievement to share.

The external demands placed on you by your congregation, your staff and the community burden you like bags of cement on your shoulders. I once had such a controlling boss he would call me at 8:01 A.M. or 4:59 P.M. to see if I were at my desk. Given such circumstances, sometimes a pastor can feel like he's standing in the middle of an hourglass. The sand pouring from the top squeezes you in the middle and the open funnel at the bottom is pouring out to everyone else.

In I Kings 19, we see our calling-down-fire-from-heaven hero, Elijah, in an old-fashioned funk. He descended from his Mt. Carmel victory to a valley of depression. He went from his best to his worst. He fumbled from faith to fear. He moved from confronting 450 prophets of Baal to running from one woman. If we aren't careful, we can succumb to the same despondency. Elijah felt alone and ready to die. How did a prophet with such a holy pedigree come to this?

Fear Feeds Loneliness

Elijah's first mistake was getting ahead of God. Less than twenty-four hours earlier, he witnessed the flames of Jehovah fall at Mt. Carmel. He watched in amazement as the dormant spiritual fuse of the apathetic Israelites was ignited by a display of God's power and they dispatched the prophets of Baal.

Then, Jezebel threatened his life. She was clearly incensed and the vitriol fairly dripped from each letter of the message she sent to her nemesis: "May the gods deal with me, be it ever so severely, if by this time tomorrow I do not make your life like that of one of them" (v. 2). This was not one of those anonymous letters pastors receive with no return address. Jezebel wanted Elijah to know she put a price on his head.

The revival sweeping Israel apparently stopped at the door of Ahab and his wicked wife in Jezreel. Inexplicably, Elijah ran there after the slaying of Baal's prophets. Perhaps he was hoping Jezebel would repent. After operating in murder, immorality, control, and a spirit of manipulation, would she change after hearing of God's powerful display? Elijah was disappointed. In fact, the Scripture says, "Elijah was afraid and ran for his life" (v. 3).

An Inward Focus Feeds Loneliness

Elijah's second mistake was looking at circumstances instead of the Lord. After running even further to Beersheba, "he left his servant there, while he himself went a day's journey into the desert. He came to a broom tree, sat down under it and prayed that he might die. 'I have had enough, Lord,' he said. 'Take my life; I am no better than my ancestors'" (vv. 3-4). Earlier in this story, it was not unusual for Elijah to be alone, but now, for the first time, his solitude caused him to shift from an outward focus to an inward focus. By sprinting to Beersheba, he was now 150 miles from Jezebel and Jezreel, but God never instructed him to run. Elijah also decided he needed no one and deserted his servant. He was alone and he was ready to quit.

The adrenaline rush from the mountaintop victory at Carmel vanished as quickly as a bite of cotton candy. It's amazing how we rationalize ungodly spiritual behavior when we're alone. In the depths of his emotional pit, Elijah "prayed that he might die" (v. 4).

Exhaustion Feeds Loneliness

You think your pastoral schedule is tough? Examine closely all Elijah accomplished in a compressed period of time:

1. The all-day public encounter on Mt. Carmel.

2. The Baal prophets were executed.

3. Elijah climbed back to Carmel for a time of intense prayer for rain to return.

4. Elijah's servant spotted a cloud on the horizon as small as a man's hand. God answered his prophet's prayers.

5. Elijah ran the seventeen to twenty miles to Jezreel.

What are the tell-tale signs of despondency? Feeling emotionally, physically and spiritually drained are clues. Minirth and his colleagues (1) defined burnout as "the letdown that comes in between crises or directly after 'mission accomplished.'" That is precisely what happened to Elijah. The queen threatened his life so he ran 150 miles to Beersheba. In addition, the Scripture says he left his servant and walked a day's journey into the desert. God didn't put all this on him. Elijah, a man of prayer, made these decisions while ignoring his Maker. If you want to really multiply your depression, run a marathon, refuse the company of friends, and head to a desolate, hot, and arid place. He was so exhausted from all this he lay down under a tree and fell fast asleep (vv. 5-6).

Lack of Relationships Feeds Loneliness

Elijah mistakenly expected Jezebel to repent, but do we see any evidence God gave Elijah permission to confront her? In fact, there's no evidence in the biblical record Elijah ever spoke directly to Jezebel. He entered a skirmish God didn't direct him to undertake. He prayed for rain, not direction to confront Jezebel. I believe if Elijah's servant had the nerve or even permission to confront his boss, Elijah might not have found himself praying to die. Relationships are so important in the life of a leader.

It's a little like Blue the mule. A traveler lost control of his car and it slid into a ditch. A farmhouse was nearby so he asked the farmer if he had a tractor he could borrow to retrieve his automobile.

"Nope, but I got a mule named Blue. He'll do," said the farmer.

"I doubt if a mule will get the job done," responded the doubtful driver.

"You don't know, Blue," replied the farmer. Blue was hitched to the car.

"Pull, Blue!" the car didn't budge. The farmer yelled, "Pull, Elmer!" The car moved a little. Then the farmer hollered, "Pull, Biscuit!" and the car was free.

"Thank you," said the car owner. "But I have a question. You called your mule by three different names. How is that?"

"Simple," said the farmer. "Blue is blind. If he thought he was the only one pulling, your car would still be in the ditch!"

If a pastor lacks relationships both inside and outside the congregation it may contribute to feelings of loneliness. Even though Abe was happily married, he lacked a consistent means of social support. Abe's brother was a pastor with whom he often sought counsel. There were also some men with whom Abe ate breakfast on a regular basis. Even though he did his best to assimilate the new families attending his church, he didn't appear to have developed strong support among them. It also appeared the breakfast group to which he referred wasn't a sufficient means of discourse to work through his feelings. He didn't mention any hobbies or clubs to which he had any affiliation, only his church.

Shortly after his promotion from a staff position to lead pastor, Chet experienced a series of catastrophes in his leadership role: the accident involving the wife of his newly-hired youth pastor, the ten-year-old boy in his congregation who attempted to hang himself, an anonymous letter criticizing the worship leader. Chet internalized the stress and isolated himself. "I didn't share much with my wife. I didn't share much with the board. I didn't share much with the staff…and I was miserable." He admitted, "I had a support group. I just didn't utilize them."

Gwen also appeared to have an absence of supportive relationships. In her interview, she made no mention of any friends coming to her aid. She never referred to a support group to which she could turn. This only heightened her distress. The ultimate evidence of this is the first year after her exit, "I stayed away from people as much as I could."

Hank enjoyed his work as a first-time senior pastor, but was not accustomed to ever being able to separate his professional life from his personal self. The loneliness was overwhelming. Even though his church was growing and he was leading the construction of an addition to the church facilities, he suffered from extreme anxiety and depression.

One of the glaring gaps Hank noticed when he moved from business to the ministry was an absence of relationships. As a successful businessman, "You had a certain respect." When introduced as a pastor, though, Hank felt an invisible wall erected by people he met. He illustrated with an upward sweep of his hand and an accompanying, "Voop! It's very hard to find real relationships. This has got to be one of the loneliest jobs I've ever had in my life."

What bothered Hank was the hidden agenda orchestrated by some church members. "A lot of people want you, but usually it's because they've got something bad happening. It's never about 'what can we do with you or help you or for you.' It's always in need of and it's always with a problem." Hank added, "Just having a real relationship with a friend is just almost impossible." He'd even gone so far as to try and find an older pastor to mentor him, "They're hard to find. I found a lot of older pastors, but not that are still vibrant."

In a *State of the Pastors* webcast on January 26, 2017, Barna Research revealed 71% of pastors are sometimes or frequently lonely. Additionally, nearly half of pastors suffer depression. Loneliness and isolation have taken its toll on the vast majority in this profession. The Barna webcast opined, "Surgeons would never spend time only with their patients."

Hank's disappointment at not being able to find a

seasoned colleague to serve as a competent mentor is a testament to some of the unfavorable consequences of serving in such a demanding vocation without the proper survival techniques.

He characterized the irony of his situation, "I mean I was running like crazy. I don't burnout. Everybody else burns out, but I don't burn out." He yearned for the understanding of his congregation, "Or I'm probably not going to be able to make it much longer."

Research reveals loneliness may be lethal. McClintock (2), a University of Chicago psychology professor announced an incredible conclusion, "The increase in morbidity with social isolation is equal to that of cigarette smoking." Although none of the participants in this study expired as a result of loneliness, nevertheless feelings of isolation compounded chronic stress for half of the interviewees.

Even though Abe had relationships outside the church, his inability or neglect to develop friendships inside the parish may have proved an impediment to a longer stay. Chet made a conscious decision to handle things alone and he resigned after one year. Gwen didn't emphasize relationships while in her senior pastor role. She chose a nearly solitary existence for eighteen months in the aftermath of her ouster – a likely factor why she wasn't able to fully recover from her experience. Hank admitted being a pastor was his loneliest job—ever!

The literature supports this as a common malady among clerics (3). Lifeway Research (4) conducted a survey of 1,000 American Protestant pastors and found fifty-five percent say being in ministry makes them feel lonely at times. Pastors are reported to often have a lack of personal friends with accompanying feelings of loneliness and isolation (5). Miller (6) explained there is "a tension felt by every minister: the tension between being a *pastor* (filling the role, performing) and being a *person* (relating to people as I am within, apart from what role I take or work I do)."

Further exacerbating the problem is the effect pastoral constraints have on clergy marriages. Hall (7) cited the findings of Warner and Carter (1984) in a study of pastors and their wives in comparison to lay persons for quality of life. Pastors experienced significantly more loneliness than those in non-pastoral roles. The researchers interpreted the results to indicate loneliness is caused by both burnout and diminished marital adjustment. Both of these are fueled by the excessive demands of the pastorate.

Hank, in particular, noted both he and his wife didn't experience this when he was an associate, but it emerged once he assumed the leadership role of senior pastor. Gwen and her husband were uninformed about their estranged son's whereabouts even though he was living with a prominent church member. They only discovered where he was living more by accident than intentional disclosure, evidence of their lack of close relationships within the church community.

Noticeable by its absence was the lack of emotional support in the midst of stress among ministerial colleagues in this study. Different participants were hesitant about sharing with others because they don't trust others when they're vulnerable. Ben asked, "Who do you trust?" Chet chose to internalize his struggle. A significant number of clients seen by Hank's counselor are pastors. "That irritates the hound out of me," he exclaimed. "Why can we not trust each other and talk about it? If we would just trust each other." Hence, the frustration is only compounded as clergy search for appropriate means to cope with both acute and chronic stress.

In I Kings 19, there are steps Elijah took both by default and by the instruction of God enabling him to overcome his loneliness.

Proper Rest and Nourishment

It's tough for anyone to make lucid decisions when tired and hungry. Elijah was so exhausted from his ordeal he lay down and fell fast asleep even in the glare of a burning desert sun. He was awakened from his slumber by an angel who provided fresh bread and clear, cool water (v. 6). He ate to his heart's content, much like the angels must have fed our Lord after his battle with Beelzebub in the wilderness (Matthew 4). After a sumptuous meal, Elijah was so relaxed he fell asleep once again. He must have been experiencing deep REM sleep because the angel served as his alarm clock once more. This time, God's messenger instructed Elijah to eat yet again in preparation for a journey of forty days and forty nights (vv. 7-8). God was moving Elijah another 150 miles, but back to Horeb, the mountain of God. He would now be 300 miles from his antagonist, Jezebel. He'd spend about six weeks traveling; it would be quality time communing with God.

Listen to the Lord

Elijah was headed back to the mountain where God spoke to Moses. "There he went into a cave and spent the night. And the word of the Lord came to him, 'What are you doing here, Elijah?'" (v. 9). Notice, this is the *first* time the word of the Lord came to Elijah in this passage. In the previous passages, the word of the Lord came early to Elijah: at Kerith, at Zarephath, and when he was to show himself a second time to Ahab in the third year of the drought. He stopped running. He was rested.

He was properly nourished and now he was ready to hear from God.

God asked Elijah a seemingly ironic question given the fact God told Elijah to travel to this location. Surprisingly, God allows His prophet to vent. Can you hear yourself in this rant? "I have been very zealous for the Lord God Almighty," replies Elijah (v. 10). He portrays himself in an uncharacteristically proud fashion while condemning his peers: "The Israelites [everyone in my church] have rejected your covenant, broken down your altars, and put your prophets to death with the sword" (v. 10).

He's suffering from selective memory loss because the Israelites just repented on Mt. Carmel. It wasn't his countrymen putting God's prophets to the sword, but Jezebel. For good measure, he reminded the Omniscient One, "I am the only one left, and now they are trying to kill me too" (v. 10). When we don't listen to God, we lose perspective:

- Didn't Obadiah tell him 100 prophets were squirreled away in a couple of caves?
- Didn't Elijah have a faithful servant do his bidding?
- Wasn't it Jezebel trying to kill Elijah and not the Jews?

God's prophet focused on lies from Satan and Jezebel instead of listening to the Lord. His comments made it clear his attitude degenerated into self-pity, resentment, dwelling on the past, and hyperbole. Do you see any similarities between Elijah's condition and those of lonely pastors?

God wanted to speak to Elijah and it would be left to God's servant as to how he would respond. "The Lord said, 'Go out and stand on the mountain in the presence of the Lord, for the Lord is about to pass by'" (v. 11). If you want God to speak to you in your loneliness, you must get to a place where He's about to pass by; a change of pace from where you are right now.

The Lord sent a "great and powerful wind" which ripped the mountains apart and shattered rocks, "but the Lord was not in the wind" (v. 11). The Lord then caused an earthquake, "but the Lord was not in the earthquake" (v. 11). Then the Lord brought a fire, "but the Lord was not in the fire" (v. 12). "And after the fire came a gentle whisper. When Elijah heard it, he pulled his cloak over his face and went out and stood at the mouth of the cave" (vv. 12-13).

Will you please look closely at the Scripture? What did God command Elijah to do at the outset? "Go out and stand on the mountain in the presence of the Lord." Notice, Elijah stayed in the cave. He didn't obey the Lord's instruction. What was God's response? "Okay, Elijah, you want the spectacular, I'll give you spectacular: wind, an earthquake, a fire," but the Lord was not present in any of them. It's not the Lord is averse to the spectacular. The Holy Spirit is like the wind, blowing where it chooses (John 3:8). Paul and Silas were rescued from prison by a God-induced earthquake. Soldiers guarding the tomb of Christ were alarmed when an earthquake moved the stone. God sent fire to Mt. Carmel and on the day of Pentecost.

It was only when Elijah heard the gentle whisper of God he emerged from his cave. Perhaps, in the midst of your search for the spectacular, you've missed God's whisper.

Focus on the Solution

Elijah was focused on the problem. God was focused on a solution. Once again, the question is asked of the prophet, "What are you doing here, Elijah?" (v. 13). Seeming a bit like a chastened child, Elijah gives the same reply he offered earlier, but it doesn't seem to have the same sarcasm. Maybe he was hoping God would send the wind, earthquake and fire to consume Jezebel! More than 150 years ago, the German poet, Heinrich Heine, wrote, "My wishes are a humble dwelling with a thatched roof, a good bed, good food, flowers at my windows, and some fine tall trees before my door. And if the good God wants to make me completely happy, He will grant me the joy of seeing six or seven of my enemies hanging from those trees." As a pastor, you can't stay focused on the problem or the people causing your stress.

Notice the progression of steps God gave to Elijah. First, he needed proper rest and nourishment. Second, he needed an extended amount of time alone with God. Elijah was effective in his ministry when he was focused on the Lord and God was able to remind him in the midst of impossible circumstances He was still in control. Third, God allowed Elijah the opportunity to vent. As he did, Elijah realized he was focused on the past, had lost perspective, and it manifested in exaggerations. By the way, researchers have discovered pounding your head against a wall for one hour will burn 150 calories. You may feel like pounding your head against a wall some times, but I don't recommend it. There are healthier ways to vent to God and lose 150 calories at the same time.

Cultivate Relationships

The fourth and final step is critical to resolving the issue of loneliness for a pastor. God used the moment to realign Elijah with His purposes. He gave him some new tasks, but these were focused on recruiting new help in the battle. God didn't expect Elijah to carry the fight to the enemy alone. His first assignment was to anoint Hazael as king over Aram (v. 15). This would solve an international conundrum because Hazael would succeed Ben-Hadad. Ben-Hadad was Israel's perennial adversary in Damascus.

His next ally on a national level would be Jehu. God wanted Elijah to be proactive and anoint Jehu as the next king over Israel. Ahab and Jezebel's days as the Israelite monarchs were numbered. These were simple tasks assigned by God.

God knows how much we can take and this led to Elijah's third recruit. Elisha was to be commissioned by Elijah as his successor. That meant Elijah would assume the role of mentor and his legacy would be established through the next generation. This gave Elijah hope as well as an additional relationship.

Notice how God provided Elijah with a fresh vision. The Lord assured His servant Jehu would put to death any who escape the sword of their ally in Damascus (v. 17). Elisha would kill anyone who escaped the sword of Jehu (v. 17). The real blessing for Elijah was Elisha would become his best friend, his fellow worker, and a disciple. Just for good measure, the Lord added, "Yet I reserve seven thousand in Israel – all whose knees have not bowed down to Baal and all whose mouths have not kissed him" (v. 18). Elijah was reminded he was not alone.

Gladwell (8) found extraordinarily successful people across various disciplines always have help to achieve. He concluded, "no one – not rock stars, not professional athletes, not software billionaires, and not even geniuses – ever makes it alone" (p. 115).

CHAPTER 8

Primary Preventions

"If you are traveling with a child or someone who requires assistance, secure your mask first and then assist the other person" (Inflight Safety Demonstration).

Forestry experts (1) employ "prescribed fire" techniques to reduce hazardous fuels and prevent catastrophic fires. Prescribed burning is "fire applied in a knowledgeable manner to forest fuels on a specific land area under selected weather conditions to accomplish predetermined, well-defined management objectives." A prescribed burn prevents the growth of "ladder fuels" like small white fir trees growing under larger ones. It exposes mineral soil for seedbeds for regeneration of wind-disseminated species, improves wildlife and livestock habitat, and helps control insects. The first stage of managing your stress is the elimination of "ladder fuels" in your life.

Mark Owen (2) learned primary preventive measures in his Navy SEAL training. Along with his fellow candidates, they learned "to be comfortable being uncomfortable." SEALS (3) learn to overcome cold, exhaustion, fear, stress, and pain because it's "easy to lose focus, drive, and determination, when things are uncomfortable" (3). One unique SEALS exercise is the hooded box test. A hood with a rope tied to it is attached to a pulley system. When the instructors yank the rope, the hood comes off and the SEAL must react to the scenario. While under the hood, he doesn't know if he has to react to a hostage situation, unarmed but violent bystanders, or handle compliant individuals who could become hostile in a split second. The scenario might be something the SEAL never encountered previously, but it's specifically designed to overwhelm the candidate, forcing the trainee to make the right decision under enormous stress and pressure. Each SEAL must quickly assess the situation, prioritize threats, and act accordingly.

Both the forestry service and the Navy SEALS are proactive in preventive measures. Engineers have certain design principles they utilize, one of which is engineering solutions to problems must precede the problem. Stress is as much a part of your occupation as ladder fuels, assessing situations, and engineering solutions before there's a problem. You learned how to construct a sermon and administer the Sacraments. If you're going to survive and thrive in the ministry, you must learn to manage your stress.

The seasoned pastors in this study revealed eleven coping strategies:

1. A clear, divine call to the profession

2. Family support

3. Prayer

4. Relationships

5. Retreats

6. Scripture

7. Reading

8. Visiting a counselor

9. Exercise

10. A weekly day off

11. Leadership development

As a pastor, your decision to adopt a particular coping program may impact your future in the profession. Based on the research, the chart on the next page illustrates the tendency toward a longer pastorate may be connected to a greater number of coping strategies.

	Abe	Ben	Chet	Donna	Evan	Frank	Gwen	Hank
Calling	Abe	Ben	Chet	Donna	Evan	Frank	Gwen	Hank
Family	Abe	Ben		Donna	Evan	Frank		Hank
Prayer	Abe	Ben		Donna	Evan	Frank		Hank
Relationships	Abe	Ben		Donna	Evan	Frank	Gwen	
Retreats		Ben	Chet	Donna	Evan	Frank		Hank
Scripture	Abe	Ben		Donna		Frank		Hank
Reading		Ben	Chet		Evan		Gwen	
Counselor			Chet		Evan		Gwen	Hank
Exercise		Ben	Chet		Evan	Frank		
Day off				Donna	Evan	Frank		
Leadership Development		Ben		Donna		Frank		
Total Coping Strategies	5	9	5	8	9	9	4	6

These results also indicate clergy may engage at different levels in the use of coping behaviors. The extent to which the participants employed coping strategies was classified into three categories: passively-engaged, moderately-engaged, and competently-engaged.

The *passively-engaged used five or fewer coping processes.* These individuals were either ignorant of the value of coping strategies or chose to ignore them. The result was difficulty moderating stress, thereby increasing the potential to abruptly end one's ministerial career. Chet, Abe and Gwen implemented the least number of coping methods. They had the most abbreviated terms of service. Each of them also exited the position of lead pastor.

The *moderately-engaged used six or seven coping processes*. At the time of his interview, Hank was the sole practitioner with six mechanisms. His tenure was longer than those in the first category. He confessed to a desperate need for help to mediate his excessive demands. Hank vacillated about adding coping strategies. He was reluctant to take the necessary time from his schedule. I ran into one of Hank's colleagues two years after our interview. The friend informed me Hank allegedly left his wife and the ministry and entered the world of business.

The *competently-engaged used eight or more coping processes*. Donna, Evan, Frank and Ben employed a plethora of behaviors. The result produced a sustaining effect on their ability to endure in the midst of both chronic and acute stressors. They recognized the value of moderating stress aggressively and appropriately. From his years of professional experience, Evan learned to structure coping devices into his life. Even though he was diagnosed with compassion fatigue, "I think my salvation was having those resources built into my life ahead of time." He further emphasized, "I need to take care of me spiritually, personally, emotionally, and the best way for me was contact with other pastors."

Frank concurred, "At age forty-seven, it's finally sinking into my thick head that self-care is absolutely paramount. If I don't take care of me no one's going to take care of me and if I'm not in good shape then what good am I to anybody?"

You are responsible for you! You may not have control over the stressors you encounter, but you certainly can develop coping strategies to slow things down. Research suggests primary prevention as well as secondary and tertiary interventions are necessary to mediate stress (4).

Primary prevention is anticipatory. Leadership development and relationships fall into this category. The pastors who developed leadership teams and relationships were more apt to have staying power. The two frequently worked together to deflect criticism of the pastor and afforded delegation of responsibility, thereby lessening the time and work constraints on the minister.

Leadership Development

Leadership development involves assessing, recruiting and training individuals to assume a wide variety of duties within the congregation. The church becomes more effective and efficient while easing the burden on the pastor. Even Jesus knew He couldn't do ministry alone.

Ben, Donna and Frank modeled this approach. Their years of experience and training as well as the necessity of delegation to ease stress bore fruit. This trio also had three of the longest tenures of those in the study.

Ben tried not only to move a congregation from one property to another, but to raise the necessary funds to build the new facilities. All of this entailed changing the mindset of the members. "The point was to build for additional ministry," he stated. Leadership development caused stress to resolve, "Who is going to be the leader?" He began with specific plans and a vision. "I wanted to have women's ministry, youth ministry, ministry to men and the families, evangelism, discipleship, all those kinds of things to develop people." He met resistance because his plan wasn't supported by some of the Old Guard leaders.

As a result, "I started developing leadership around me," he said. He invested himself in "three, ten, or twelve men and women, teenagers, whoever." He influenced them to do ministry. He always spent time with people. Prayer ministry was a key area of leadership development. "Prayer is really what did something to the atmosphere of our church." People began to join the church and, in turn, it grew. He worked in small groups where they "minister to you as well as you minister to them." In his view, he kept doing the same things he felt were the right priorities and a mission fit. After nearly twenty-five years at his church, Ben was still excited about leadership development. His "greatest joy" has been developing leaders: "You know, this is what I always wanted my church to be, total ministry to total man...to the total person." His years of investment paid great dividends not only for his church, but for the community. Those raised in his church came back to be schoolteachers, attorneys, and doctors in the community. "I have kids who are really contributing to the fiber of America and that's the kind of stuff that motivates me to continue."

"I would be so uptight and couldn't sleep," said Donna. Just a year prior to our interview, she attended a continuing education seminar for pastors in her denomination. The seminar leaders "helped me learn to say, 'No.'" After taking the class, she decided to make significant changes in her leadership style. "I've started to handle things differently." Donna concluded, "I don't feel I need to be at every meeting. That's why you have committees and chair people." Donna had one of her leaders tell her, "Don't come. You don't need to be here. You know if there's anything to be taken care of we will tell you."

As far as ministry in the church is concerned, she

suggested, "You find people that have those gifts and graces and you give responsibility to them." She reasoned, "There are things I can do well and there are things I don't do well and there are other people in the church who do them well. So why am I trying to do it and not being very successful?"

Frank saw the importance of learning leadership development from experts. He attended seminars by Eason Bandy and John Maxwell. Frank credited his grandmother who lived with his family for nineteen years in understanding his "older generation" of members. Those lessons served him well as a rookie with a number of elderly parishioners. Frank focused on building a lot of trust with them: "They became my key 'circle the wagon' people as I call them." He was grateful for their support because the "circle the wagon" people "would help keep a lot of the alligators and troublemakers under control."

Frank was a solo pastor, but had a parish nurse to whom he delegated a lot of responsibility. "She has been a true blessing as far as hospital visitations and things." The parish nurse had a team of volunteers whose responsibilities included ministry to shut-ins. He made it a point to build upon that "foundation for what needs to transpire in the future." Based on their study of thousands of leaders, Tichy and Bennis (5) emphasized "winning leaders are teachers. They drive their organizations through teaching, and they develop others to be leaders/teachers." They characterized this as Teachable Points of View. "TPOVs are what enable leaders to take the valuable knowledge and experience they have stored up inside their heads and teach them to others" (6). It contributes to enlisting and energizing others to make the proper decisions and fulfill the vision. Greenleaf (7) characterized clergy as "servant–leaders" who wish to help others to "a larger and nobler vision and purpose than they would be likely to attain for themselves."

Since the church is considered a non-profit organization comprised primarily of volunteers with varying levels of commitment as well as skill-sets, it represents challenges for the most experienced leader. Leadership shouldn't be considered an individual work because in the church "Lone Ranger" leadership can prove to be a fatal mistake. Abe, Chet, and Gwen were all victimized by neglecting leadership development and the result was tumultuous and abbreviated pastorates.

When a minister assumes the pulpit of a local church, he or she is only granted a title as the leader. Developing leadership allows the pastor to gain currency more quickly among the membership as he or she invests in the production of leadership teams. Frank illustrated this principle with both his college exchange student experience and his seminary internship in eastern Pennsylvania. Frank learned to respect traditions and "learn the language" in both settings. The experiences served him well as an "ouslander," to coin a Dutch term, and those principles carried into his ministry. He learned the value of working with key influencers to move the congregation in the proper direction.

Relationships

There are two categories of relationships a pastor should develop. The first are internal advocates. These are the "take a bullet for you" people in your church. They affirm you, run interference with troublemakers, and they love you enough to admonish you if you're on thin ice. The greater the number of supportive relationships in the congregation and the more satisfied the pastor is with these relationships, the more positive is his or her attitude (8).

Relationships are highly valued for clergy with extended parish tenures. To have persons both individually and collectively upon whom they can rely for moral support and advice is imperative. When an individual is engaged in a high stress environment, affirmation from friends, family and neighbors is necessary to provide support and nurture. Social support is an important buffer to blunt the adverse effects work stress may have on one's health (9).

The summer after high school, the BMOC and I became

great friends. We played tennis, went swimming and chased girls. We both looked forward to college in the fall. He was armed with a scholarship to play basketball. I started flirting with Sasha*. She was a couple years younger and going steady with an underclassman. Her boyfriend, Todd*, was upset I asked Sasha for a date. One evening, the BMOC and I were playing tennis when Todd came roaring to the court on his bike. He was so mad he could've chewed nails and spit out a barbed wire fence. He yelled from his bike, "You won't mess with my girlfriend anymore!" He dismounted his bike and headed in my direction. When someone is in such a state, they don't always think clearly. For one, Todd ignored the fact I held a tennis racquet in my hand. For another, the BMOC had my back. He never moved in Todd's direction. He simply, clearly and forcefully said, "If you're going to do anything to him, you'll have to come through me!" Todd turned on his heels, mounted his bike and left. He never bothered me again.

Every pastor needs some BMOC's. It doesn't happen automatically. Just like my high school friend, you have to spend time with people. Share meals, make memories, do projects together. Laugh, cry and pray together. These advocates should be a by-product of your leadership development. They recognize the need to defend and support the shepherd of the flock.

In Ben's case, "The former pastor's son was one of my greatest supporters." This is unusual since former pastors, their spouses and family members who remain in the congregation can often be hostile to the new pastor and any changes. There was also a gentleman who served as the deacon chair who loved Ben and his family. Ben also counted an older wealthy lady who hosted Ben's family many times and served as a confidante.

Donna explained, "I have a group of about three gals that have been real good in a covenant group. We meet on Wednesdays for prayer for about an hour and I do a study with them occasionally, a book study." Donna noted, "This is unusual in that these are members of my congregation, but it's a safe place." She intimated, "They see a lot of things because they are very active in the church and they have kind of smoothed, sometimes, hurt feelings." Donna has no hesitation about being transparent with these ladies. Their value has been in prayer, moral support, and they've intervened with members of the congregation who didn't agree with her.

The second category of relationships is external advisers. A lack of trust is a factor in why some pastors don't confide to people in their congregation. A pastor needs to have some form of social support in order to maintain his or her well-being (10). Ben relied upon colleagues and friends living outside the state for advice from time to time. Thanks to a grant through his denomination, Evan along with four other pastors submitted a proposal for continuing education to the Lilly Foundation. The two-year grant paid for lunches and books in a retreat setting. Evan said, "The typical format was for about four hours we'd have a presentation and we'd talk...about issues." Even though the grant expired, "We just keep meeting." In this group, they are transparent enough with one another to ask, "How are you doing personally, spiritually, and professionally?" For both Donna and Evan, these groups were places of refuge not just to vent, but for solace in the midst of difficult circumstances.

I assumed the pastorate of a church in 2009 and less than two years later, my world imploded. The congregation was very gracious to me, but I was an emotional mess. I sought wisdom from friends, but I needed more. I fasted and prayed, but I needed more. I went to a professional counselor, but I needed more than one hour a week to process things. Then I attended an appreciation luncheon for pastors and met David Ward. A retired technology genius, David had a heart for pastors. His Pastor Advisory Council (PAC) was in its infancy when he invited me to attend a meeting. He not only gave me a brochure at the luncheon, he followed up with a visit to my office. I didn't share everything I was experiencing, but David sensed I needed encouragement. When he came to my office, I figured he was selling something, but he surprised me.

"I meet monthly with a group of pastors at a country club. We start at 9 AM and finish about 4 PM. Lunch and snacks are provided. There's no charge for the initial visit. Just come one time and see what you think."

How could I resist a free lunch at a country club? I decided to go–just one time. I made sure my calendar was clear and made my way to the country club. It was beautifully appointed. I entered the meeting room and saw about eight casually-dressed guys gathered around a conference table. Tea, juice, coffee and pastries sat on a credenza. Everybody had a cardboard name plate on the table in front of them. I sat at the spot designated for me with a folder, pen, highlighter, notepad, and Post-it Notes. The first paper in the folder was the covenant for members of PAC. Everyone could share transparently, but what was shared in the room, stayed in the room. You couldn't tell your best friend or your spouse what was discussed. None of this was to be sermon illustration fodder or social media gossip. If you had any of those inclinations, you didn't belong in this group.

David had an agenda, but was flexible. A brief devotional, leadership discussions, and prayer time were followed by a lunch buffet. In the afternoon, we had open sharing. I sat in silence as I listened to these fellow pastors share what was happening in their church or their personal lives. This was a profound revelation: I wasn't the only one! The other pastors would offer words of encouragement. They gave advice if solicited. Everybody had a chance to share. If you didn't want to share, there was no pressure. When all was finished, David turned to me, "Bill, do you have anything you want to share?"

I didn't take long for the tears to flow. For some reason, I felt safe with this group of strangers, and I poured forth my sorrow. When I finished, David said, "Let's gather around Bill and pray over him."

Every one of those men laid hands on me and prayed over me. It was the equivalent of taking a spiritual bath. I knew this was a vital component missing in my life.

I accepted David's invitation to join the group on a monthly basis. There was a financial commitment, but David didn't let money stand in the way of participation. I don't think I'm exaggerating when I say this group helped save my life and my ministry. I never had a confidence betrayed. I always felt safe with these men. The group changed over the years, but not the core principles.

Every pastor needs an outside group of confidantes for venting, for different perspectives, and as a refuge in a storm. A pastor needs a safe place to laugh and relax and not have to be "on."

Frank learned the value of external advisers, "I like to talk things over with people. I have friends who are not pastors who are not in this community that I can call." When he moved to his new parish, "I had a buddy I met when I moved here and we hit it off." This was a colleague with whom he confided and built a great relationship. Even their families built a connection.

Once Gwen left the pastorate and worked through her grief, she gradually added relationships. Gwen now has a female accountability partner with whom she meets every other week. Their accountability and respect is mutual, "She ... makes me feel purposeful in helping another person." She is also part of a "women in ministry group" in her home denomination and participates in a multi-denominational women's ministry group. These ladies are able to share their experiences, empathize and offer advice as females in ministry.

The value of venting in a safe place or to a trusted confidante cannot be understated for preachers. Engaging a trusted confidante about self-doubt, important decisions, or critical self-assumptions was advantageous in alleviating stress.

Moses illustrated the value of relationships with Aaron and Hur in Exodus 17:11-12. Every time Moses lifted his staff, the Israelites prevailed in their battle with the Amalekites. When he dropped his staff, the Amalekites prevailed. When Moses grew tired, it was Aaron and Hur who put a stone under him so he could sit. They were at his side to hold up his arms so he could continue to raise his staff. The Israelites defeated their enemy, but God provided a palpable object lesson for his children and future generations. God's leader needs help. He needs relationships with those who will come alongside to win victories in the life of a church.

CHAPTER 9

Secondary Interventions

"A teachable spirit is more important than a fighting spirit"

(Unknown).

History teaches the value of preventive measures. After a fire destroyed ancient Rome in 64 A. D., Emperor Nero rebuilt the city with wider public avenues, limitations in building heights, provision of fireproof construction and improvements to the city water supplies.

A catastrophic fire at the Cleveland Clinic on May 15, 1929, began when an exposed light bulb, located too close to some nitro-cellulose x-ray film, ignited the film. The 123 deaths included patients, visitors, employees, and one of the founders of the famous clinic, Dr. John Phillips. Most victims died from inhaling poisonous gases. The Cleveland fire influenced major changes at both the local and national levels. The City of Cleveland decided fire departments should receive gas masks as part of their equipment and advocated creating an ambulance service for the city. Nationally, medical facilities established new standards for storing hazardous materials such as x-ray film.

For clergy, secondary interventions include the calling to the profession, prayer, Scripture, reading, exercise, and a day off. All the subjects made daily decisions about whether or not to participate in any of these. Obviously, an emergency could interrupt a day or illness and injury would prevent exercise.

The symptoms generated by clergy stress or any kind of chronic stress are pretty clear. Chances are you become increasingly irritable. In 2014, the *European Heart Journal* released a study linking heart attacks to angry outbursts. An angry person increased the chances of a heart attack by eight and-a-half times within the next two hours. The angry outbursts could be accompanied by elevated blood pressure, increased heart rate, tightening of the blood vessels, and increased clotting (1).

It reminds me of my days as a youth pastor. Often, we headed to a beautiful campground for a week of ministry to our students. Teenagers can be needy people. One particular year, it was a difficult camp. Every time I turned around it seemed someone wanted something or was asking me a question. By Friday, I'd had it up to my eyeballs with questions. I was eating breakfast with the guest speaker when I said, "So help me, if one more kid asks me a question I think I'll have to …"

Just then Ryan tapped me on the shoulder and started, "Pastor Bill…"

I interrupted. "Ryan, I don't know what you're about to say, but whatever it is, it better not be a question. You can say anything you want to me; just make sure you don't put it in the form of a question!"

With big innocent eyes he responded, "Like what?"

Additional signs of chronic stress include feeling obsessed about work, driven by a constant sense of urgency, anxiety, a lack of energy and loss of creativity. When I've been overwhelmed by my responsibilities and the accompanying emotional demands, I can stare at my Bible or my computer and wonder how I am going to preach to people this week. If not carefully managed, stress can lead to the decision to simply quit. Secondary interventions are stabilizers or corrective in nature. Deciding to make this part of your lifestyle may be rougher than sitting on a pine cone toilet seat, but you need to take action.

Divine Call

Surgeons or teachers may view their vocation as a calling, ministers perceive theirs as a divine edict. For most, this event takes on almost mystical dimensions, but is necessary to endure the uncertainties of the ministry. Each of the eight participants noted a divine call and identified how it was an artifice of stability when faced with uncertainty.

Abe felt called when he was twelve years old. Ben received his call while in high school. Chet came to the realization "being involved in ministry is more than just serving as a pastor in a church...that's helped me in creating who I am today as I seek to equip people." Donna acknowledged her call later in life.

Frank, Evan, and Hank mentioned they weren't eager to follow the call initially, which is not uncommon for some pastors. Evan initially resisted his call with the dismissive thought of "what a way to ruin your life." Yet, "it's like God won't leave me alone," he said, and he eventually pursued his chosen vocation. He was happy in the decision because "life's been very smooth." His life experiences affirmed his career choice.

Frank wasn't warm to following in his father's footsteps. After attending a performance of Handel's *Messiah* in St. Mary's Cathedral in Scotland, he went for a walk in the snow. He wistfully recollected the memory with fondness, and "really felt God's touch, God's saying, 'You need to go into the pastorate.'" He pondered for "about fifteen, twenty seconds and then said, 'Nah,'" he laughingly recalled. When he returned to a university, a course in Basic Christian Teachings was pivotal in his life: "I felt a fire lit within me." His ministry, even in difficult times, has affirmed his gifts and his call.

Gwen responded to her call in junior high, but didn't actively pursue it until young adulthood. She didn't necessarily resist; there were just other priorities in her life and entering the vocation as a female would be to serve as a pioneer in her denomination. Even as she described the pain of her experience at her church, she refused to deny the call on her life.

Hank was called as a teenager, but worked in churches only as a volunteer or part-time while establishing a successful career in business. "To some degree it was a lot easier [in business], but I was miserable," he laughed. Despite his struggles in the ministry, "I can't get over that I know God's called me." Despite the rookie pressures of his burgeoning church and leading his first building project, his call sustained him. "I have a confidence. There was a stake. It was driven in the ground 'cause I knew the time of doubt would come and that stake is in the ground and I know God's in it."

Despite the individual trauma each of these pastors experienced, they courageously endured because of a core belief God called him or her not only into the ministry, but to the particular place of service. If God was faithful to call them, He would be faithful to empower them. Miller (2) wrote, "A sense of divine call is the great slab of bedrock upon which ministry rests." Hank referred to "the ultimate sacrifice" when he responded to the call because he "actually began to follow God" then. In his first two years in the ministry, he was invited repeatedly to return to the business world. One particularly lucrative offer was well into six figures. He described a conversation in which God asked him, "Are you going to do what you're comfortable with or are you finally going to trust Me and step out there and …be the pastor I've called you to be?" Hank immediately determined to "surrender" and "give it everything I've got. I'm going to work as hard as I did when I started my business."

None in the study, regardless of circumstances, revoked his or her call. This is consistent with Greenfield's assessment if one's call was "valid and real in the beginning, it is still valid and real today. It may simply need reworking, redirecting, and renewal" (3). Chet could attest to this since he recognized his gifts were better suited for an associate rather than senior pastor.

Prayer

King David, Daniel and other Old Testament characters believed prayer to be part of the main business of life. Jesus would often get away to a solitary place to make supplication. He taught His disciples to pray. Therefore, ministers are expected to not only teach Christ-followers how to pray, but they should be regularly engaged in the practice. Three-quarters of the participants mentioned it as a resource.

Ben admitted he did "a lot of praying." Not only did he practice personal prayer time, but "prayer is really what did something to the atmosphere of our church." A plethora of intercessory events included all-night and all-day prayer vigils and forty days of fasting. The latter was also a method of personal discipline. "I did a lot of fasting…at least three days a week, every week. It cleaned me out emotionally. My mind was clear. It gave me a calm spirit and, of course, I felt better." IFA President, Gary Bergel, discovered historical and scriptural records revealed regular, even twice-a-week fasting, was a common discipline among leaders and believers in the early church (Acts 13:2, 14:23). In Ben's case, fasting enabled him not to return the vitriol aimed his direction, but instead to rise above the fray and maintain a proper perspective. Ben confessed, "[Prayer] is what motivated me, encouraged me and relieved a lot of the stress in me because I saw lives change. I saw behaviors change in a lot of people."

Before he became the senior pastor, Chet "was consistently not only spending my personal time with the Lord, but I was consistently getting away—a half day or a day a month of refueling and refreshing and reevaluating my ministry." He admitted prayer time was very important to him, but as he became more engrossed in the calamities surrounding the church, he allowed this priority to slide. Looking back, he realized it was a mistake not to spend more time in intercession.

Donna and Frank both pray while driving. Frank will pray if he wakes up early "just lying there in bed or when I'm waiting to go to sleep, when I'm sitting at the desk, sometimes in the sanctuary." He will pray while he's exercising. Whether it's lifting weights, using an elliptical machine, or practicing forms in karate, "that is excellent prayer time for me as well."

Evan meets with a small group of pastors to intercede every Wednesday morning for an hour. Journaling is Hank's form of speaking and listening to God. "The only way I really have found …prayer to be most effective is through journaling, through actually writing my prayer." He does it before and after he reads the Bible in his devotional time. Traditional forms of kneeling or being in a secluded place weren't as important as simply using prayer to mediate stress.

Every pastor may have a target or limit on how much time is spent in prayer, but research uncovered at least twenty minutes of meditation is necessary to reap the full benefits (4). A study of seventy-eight counselors, doctors, nurses and volunteers who worked in Arizona hospice programs found there was little tendency to adopt a fixed position or particular location, but it was a significant activity of everyday life, "an act of communication with a higher being on a personal level" (5).

A minister is considered God's spokesperson. Prayer helps clergy unblock awareness of God because "to get our breath we need to hope, and prayer helps us envision that hope" (6). Prayer and meditation improve both concentration and creativity (7). Hulme (8) reminded ministers facing stress: "Meditation is a way of listening to the Spirit, of observing God's hand in our life, of slowing the frenetic pace of our minds, of being still in the presence of God."

Scripture

My brother and I convinced my parents to take our travel-trailer to the lake and park it. My parents loved to camp. Their philosophy meant we always went someplace different almost every day of vacation. We hooked up the trailer, drove several miles, found a campground, unhooked the trailer, learned the location of the swimming pool, community showers and toilets and settled in for the night. The next day, we'd do it again.

As kids, we wanted to go to a lake and stay put instead of drive every day. We finally got our wish. Our parents took us to a lake in northern Indiana and we parked the trailer for the week. Dad loved to fish. For some unknown reason, he loved to go before the fish had breakfast.

The first day of vacation, instead of my brother and I

sleeping in, Dad jolted us from bed early to get in the boat, on the water, with fishing lines appropriately baited and cast. It was a waste of time. None of us had so much as a nibble on a line. In disgust, my Dad abruptly said, "Boys, we didn't have devotions before we left today. We're heading back to shore!" We reeled in our lines, made for the shore, then to the trailer, and Dad took out his Bible. As was his custom, he would read us a passage of Scripture and then pray for us.

I don't remember us fishing later. What I do remember is the consistency my mom and dad showed in their reading the Bible every day. It was a daily dose of spiritual vitamins and a stress mediator. Dad revered the Word so much, he taught us never to set anything on top of it. To the best of my knowledge, Dad read the Word daily apart from his weekly sermon preparation. Both are practices I've emulated and try to pass along to my children.

The Bible is the chief means by which people learn not only how to fellowship with God, but to gain a richer understanding of life and the imperfect world in which we live. Expositors of the Word must be able to communicate these truths to their congregations on a weekly basis. It's not only necessary to communicate its truths, but to set an example in both word and deed of following its precepts.

Even though Abe was out of the ministry, he hadn't

forsaken the Bible as a resource. While Abe continued to process the events and awaited the opportunity to return to the pastorate, he cited Psalm 138:8, "'God will perfect the things that concern me' and I believe that." The Bible was a lens through which he viewed his difficult experience.

Ben subtly credits his longevity with character studies, "because a lot of biblical models of people just stay through the battle…whatever happened." How could Ben do any less than the examples set for him in the Bible he preached every week?

As Donna prepares for a sermon it's "the weekly Scripture I live and that's what I meditate on and think about as I'm putting a sermon together." Donna didn't separate her personal devotional time from her sermon preparation. For her, the two were inexorably linked. If a passage speaks to her in a significant way during the week, she uses it as her inspiration for her message on Sunday.

Hank sees his devotional time as separate from his sermon preparation. The Scriptures served as a source of wisdom. Hank unequivocally stated, "I can't imagine what would happen if I didn't have God's Word, if I didn't have the journaling, if I didn't have the relationship" with God. Hank confessed "[if] I find myself getting weak, find myself not being in the Word" then all the expectations and demands of his profession "can drive me absolutely insane."

Foster (9) cautioned against combining personal devotions with sermon preparation. "In the study of Scripture a high priority is placed upon interpretation: what it means. In the devotional reading of Scripture a high priority is placed upon application: what it means to me." Bridges (10) begins each day with thirty minutes devoted to reading the Bible "to allow it to minister to me." "An erosion of spiritual vitality sets in when the spiritual leader does not take care of her/his own relationship with God" (11).

Reading

Mental cultivation through the reading of books and periodicals proved stimulating for half the participants, especially since theological works weren't always included. Reading extra-biblical material was noted as a release and a source of practical knowledge. Tomes consumed included theology, counseling, relationships, leadership, prayer, and fiction.

Ben made it a point to read a variety of books to alleviate stress. He consumed works on counseling, relationships, prayer, and leadership. He liked the "motivational" aspects they provided. Dr. John Maxwell was one of his favorites because of the practical leadership principles offered as well as general advice for success in life and the profession. German theologian, Dietrich Bonhoeffer, was another favorite. For Ben reading was an escape because early in his ministry, "we didn't have a whole lot of money to be doing a whole lot of exquisite vacations" so reading was a form of escape.

While Chet was going through a turbulent year, "I continued to allow myself to, you know, step away on occasion by reading." It helped him moderate the stress.

Evan received an invitation from a neighboring pastor to join a book club and readily accepted. They read non-theological books, "although books that have some relevance to the theological issues" and they met once a month at a local restaurant. It endured for "close to twelve years and that has been great." He was also part of a continuing education grant provided by the Lilly Foundation in which he and two colleagues read books on specific topics for one year. One year the focus was leadership, the next was the "emerging church." Each session lasted four hours and they took turns presenting on issues related to the reading. Even though the grant expired, "we just keep meeting."

Gwen mentioned one of her "escape mechanisms" was "reading fiction." She enjoyed the opportunity to stimulate her mind. She also loved the challenge of crossword puzzles. Anything to refresh her mentally seemed appropriate.

Leatz and Stolar (12) found reading to maintain appropriate health for those in a high-stress environment. Consuming various forms of literature was viewed as one of life's "guilty pleasures." Reading books, magazines, even pamphlets are recommended as a stress management skill (13).

A national study of 128 superintendents from urban schools and college of education deans investigated strategies for coping with stress through self/inner development (14). Six common practices were identified with reading rated as the second most frequently mentioned diversion. The diversity of interests included not only some of the same topics as the participants in this study, but biographies, news, and poems as well. The purpose was to discover ways to blunt burnout among leaders. As simple as it may sound, poring over books is an inexpensive and stimulating diversion from the strains of work.

Exercise

According to an article in the *New York Times* by Paul Vitello (August 1, 2010), clergy suffer from obesity, hypertension and depression at higher rates than the national norm. According to Vitello, clergy use of antidepressants has risen during the past decade and clergy life expectancy has fallen! O. S. Hawkins, President of Guidestone Financial Resources, stated: "Stress, lack of exercise, and poor eating habits affect more than their [ministers'] personal health. They impact their ability to do the work God has called them to do." Stress, unrealistic congregational expectations, failure to establish healthy boundaries, and the lack of consistent time off are all culprits. Dr. James Angel, professor of sports medicine at Samford University in Birmingham, Alabama, points to monitoring food intake, rest, and exercise to help maintain weight control. As a consultant to clergy, Dr. Angel has heard the excuse more than once: a minister's schedule doesn't allow time for regular aerobic exercise. Professor Angel has a classic response: "Which best fits your schedule, exercising one hour per day or being dead 24 hours per day?"

Regular exercise is a super-stress fighter for three reasons. First, exercise unleashes endorphins. These neurotransmitters support a healthy sense of well-being and optimism. Second, exercise helps block mental or emotional stress by forcing you to focus on your body and the task at hand rather than your stress. Third, exercise supports healthy sleep cycles. According to one 2014 Swiss study, people who worked out at high intensity for ninety minutes before going to bed fell asleep faster. One possible reason is vigorous exercise reduces levels of the stress hormone cortisol, a sleep saboteur, says study author Serge Brand, Ph. D., an adjunct professor with the Center for Affective, Stress, and Sleep Disorders at the University of Basel.

Additionally, regular exercise provides fuel for your body. Walking, running, and strength training can help ward off age-related bone loss. The *Healthy Mind, Healthy Body: Benefits of Exercise* report by Harvard Medical School found exercise provided as many benefits as prescription drugs for people with common conditions, such as heart disease and diabetes. The same report revealed regular exercise can boost your immune system and reduce the risk for some cancers including breast, colon and lung.

According to the June 2012 *American Journal of Preventive Medicine*, by 2030, forty-two percent of Americans will be obese. Obesity is defined by the Centers for Disease Control and Prevention as a body mass index (BMI) over 30. A five-foot, nine-inch man would be obese if he weighed 203 pounds or more. "Overweight" for a man the same height is between 169 and 202 pounds. There are many online calculators available for you to determine your BMI.

Participants in my study viewed exercise as any physical activity including walking, golfing, bicycling, lifting weights, and karate. Half of the subjects viewed exercise as a form of relief.

Ben proclaimed, "I do a lot of exercise...at least six days

a week." He walks at least five miles. Ben doesn't use headphones because he also uses the time to pray. "I like the morning time." He walks "when it's cool and not too many people out there." He walks year-round. He will even walk in "fifteen degrees outside because I don't like walking inside." He's disciplined about maintaining his regimen and it shows. Even though he was one of the older respondents, Ben was very fit and energetic.

Chet spent hours on his bicycle to alleviate stress, "For me to get on my bicycle for an hour after experiencing a day of stress is just huge. People drain me. I have to have that time." Evan goes golfing with a friend every Monday morning in the summer. He doesn't like to be alone when exercising. He and his wife regularly go for a walk in the middle of the day. This serves multiple purposes: he gets exercise, clears his mind and spends quality time with his bride. Earlier, Evan mentioned the advantage of creative scheduling as a pastor. He's not a slacker and works diligently in his profession. He's learned at his age and with his experience to arrange his schedule in such a fashion so he can handle the stress in his own time.

"Exercise is enormous for me," said Frank of his holistic approach to self-care. He exercises three times a week, participating in karate twice a week and a half hour on the elliptical or lifting weights.

No one can make you take control of your health. Pastors have demanding schedules. Still, there are steps, pardon the pun, to get moving. When you make a hospital visit, don't take the elevator, take the stairs – up as well as down. Don't park in clergy-designated areas. Park in the far reaches of a parking lot and use the walk for some simple exercise. Instead of plopping into your recliner when you come home and zoning on television, do twenty push-ups or twenty sit-ups or both. If you can't do thirty minutes of exercise at a time, do three segments of ten minutes each. You can kick a soccer ball with your kids or grandkids. You can go for a swim. Mow the lawn. Pull weeds. Just get moving!

Day Off

Clergy are often the brunt of the repeated joke they only work one day a week, but the shepherd is on call 7/24/365. The pressures seem inescapable in the ministry. Chet tried to conduct a wedding and was interrupted by a church tragedy. He attended a continuing education seminar, but he was called to another tragedy involving church members. Donna was pressured by a member for not being around enough during the Christmas holidays. Evan worked in the office on Saturdays and at least three evenings a week. Frank confessed to never working less than fifty hours a week. Both Donna and Hank admitted they are always thinking about their jobs.

Only three respondents confessed to a regular day off and they also had three of the longest pastorates in the study. It would seem a regular day away from work would be considered a primary prevention, but based on the interviews it was secondary. The fact five of the participants neglected this discipline is alarming. This may be another contributing factor to abbreviated pastorates.

"Tuesday's my day off and I do honor that because I have a new grandson," beamed Donna. She makes spending time with her family a high priority. She's reduced the number of evenings she's at church and arranges her schedule to be more available with her husband on the weekends. Evan stated, "I never work on Monday unless it's an emergency. I never work on Friday night unless it's an emergency." Frank doesn't work on Monday. His father was a pastor and Frank has only fond memories of his upbringing. The example set by his dad in using these types of methods to keep life in balance made an indelible impression upon him.

Prior to accepting the role of senior pastor, Chet took a regular day off, but once he was engaged in all the demands of a lead pastor, his plan was shredded like a top-secret government document. "I know the importance because ... number 1, I've experienced the time we did that; and number 2, I've experienced the time when I ignored it completely." It didn't cost him his health, his marriage, or his family, but it contributed to his decision to resign after one year so he could, in part, regain some control over his schedule and restore equilibrium to his life.

Congregations must understand the need for boundaries in this area for their pastor. Few churches give their pastors two full days off and ministers never have a three-day weekend (15). Saturdays are often spent in final preparation for ministers for Sunday. Saturday is also prime time for weddings, funerals, and church functions. It's unfair to ask or expect any professional to work constantly. The mind and body simply cannot function properly under those impossible demands. If a pastor's giving up his day off, let him take a "Flex Day" or "Comp Day" to spend time with his family or relax. Even Jehovah rested after creating the world in six days and commanded His followers to follow suit in Exodus 20:8-11.

The demands of a pastor require regular breaks. If God needed them, you do as well. Hank's life is a prime illustration of the disastrous consequences of one's system suffering from over-load. He didn't take a day off in his stress reduction regimen. He contemplated suicide. "Routine time off is essential for inner healing and itself is a form of spiritual retreat" (16).

CHAPTER 10

Tertiary Interventions
"The second mouse gets the cheese."

Tertiary interventions are corrective actions which include strong family support, retreats such as vacations, conferences, or sabbaticals, and the use of a professional counselor or therapist. Six pastors mentioned the affirmation of a supportive family. Ed Dobson once noted, "Resentment in a pastor's wife is like a natural gas leak—often hard to detect and discovered only after an explosion." While family can be a source of stress for a minister, their value to the participants as a source of encouragement is crucial.

Churches may not be able to afford to send their minister on a retreat or to a conference. However, those in the study who took advantage of such opportunities reaped great benefits. It was therapeutic for the pastor, and the sponsoring church witnessed a reinvigorated pastor in the pulpit. Retreats were some type of vacation or extended break from ministry responsibilities.

The use of a counselor by these pastors was beneficial. Many in the ministry see the need to project and protect a perfect image. Tommy Barnett, Pastor of Phoenix First Assembly once shared with pastors, "People need to know you have feet of clay, just don't let 'em see them." Some ministers admit a certain stigma is attached to their use of a professional counselor or therapist. Clergy are quick to refer a congregant in need of professional help, but reticent to seek the same. There's also the issue of affordability. While parishioners may have insurance companies covering the costs of a counselor, such is not always the case for a pastor. With hourly counseling rates starting at $50 and up, pastors in smaller churches may not be able to afford professional help unless their church covers the expense. Participants who engaged in therapy weren't disappointed.

Family Support

A homestead family lived "off the grid" and never saw a television much less any other modern amenities. One year, they decided on an adventure to New York City. They tried a hotel for the first time. First, they ventured into the lobby. As they were wandering around, the father and his two teenage sons noticed an elderly lady push a button on the wall. The walls parted, she stepped into a small room and the walls closed. In a minute, the walls opened again and a beautiful young woman stepped from the small room into the lobby. The boys looked wide-eyed at their father: "Dad, what just happened?" Father: "I don't know, but go get your mother!"

For Protestant pastors, a strong marriage and the support of a loving family are not only paramount for sustainability, but credibility in the community of faith. The parsonage family may experience unique strains because they are under close scrutiny. In the study, there were reports of a spouse or the children caught in the crossfire of enmity targeted against the participant or simply dealing with the effects of catastrophic events. Yet, seventy-five percent of the ministers in the study made reference to the efficacy of support from a spouse, children, parents, and siblings.

Even though Abe and his family endured a great deal in their troubled parish, both his marriage and family emerged intact. Abe appreciated his wife's support during the trials at their church, his unemployment period, and his on-going situation. As far as he's concerned, "The big parts of my life, to me the important things, are very good."

It was a mutual decision by Chet and his wife to fill the senior pastor vacancy at the church where he was employed as a staff member. Chet discussed his brief time as the lead pastor, "My wife and I had no doubt we were the ones God called to be the senior pastor." The call they sensed was an anchor for them in the midst of the immense pressure they faced. Prior to stepping into his critical role, "My wife and I had for four years been consistently dating every week, every other week." He also made it a practice to date each of his kids every four to six weeks. As senior pastor, though, "I let some stuff begin to slide" which included the dating ritual. Chet saw the value of spending time with family to mediate stress. "If I hadn't done it during the healthy times, I possibly wouldn't have survived. If I continued it during that period, we still may be there today."

Donna unequivocally stated, "If I have to take a choice between my church and my family, I'm taking my family! There's no question. I guess it's just finding the boundaries and saying, 'This is where I won't move.'" When comparing her home to her congregation, she added, "I give them 100% of who I am and then I draw the line with family time."

Evan explained one of the more creative approaches to making time for family. "I will routinely go home not just for lunch, but wander home in the morning, wander home in the afternoon, visit a little bit. We'll go take a walk in the middle of the day." He and his wife "started having our main meal at three to three-thirty in the afternoon" about five years earlier. Their children were grown so it made this practice feasible. When his kids were still in school he'd return home in the afternoon to greet them. "They'd get off the bus by say, 4:15. I'd be home by

4:15—shoot baskets with my son." They wouldn't eat until later, but he said, "Then right after supper I'd go back to church if I had something in the evening." As a pastor, Evan loved the flexibility of his daily pastoral routine. "It is one of the pluses of ministry scheduling." In his view, control over his time management "has made life seem, in many ways, more relaxing."

Frank affirmed Evan's ministry scheduling. "It creates time for vacations, time to be able to take time off to go to a certain event and such. The kids understand that's an advantage versus Daddy working a three to eleven shift and can't go to any of the school functions. So it's give and take." Frank was resolute in guarding his family. "You can pick on me, family is off limits. You start picking on my family turf, we got some real problems."

Like Abe, Hank was raised in a dysfunctional home. In his family, drug use, alcohol, prison, and his father abandoning the family cast a cloud over his formative years. Yet, he drew strength and understanding from his wife. Once Hank initiated counseling for depression, his wife accompanied him for a visit to his counselor. She learned what she could do to help. Rather than condemn him for his feelings or express dissatisfaction, she empathized with him. As they left the meeting she told Hank, "I know you, but I really didn't understand what all's really going on inside you." Her response was an emotional reprieve for Hank. He expressed gratitude and underscored the importance she knows "how to work with me."

Since all the participants were married for a substantial amount of time and all had at least two children, it stands to reason they would rely upon the affirmation of a supportive spouse and the respect of their children. When our children were young, we lived in a parsonage on the church property. We experienced an especially demanding schedule one week. So much so, one night, we posted a sign above the front doorbell: "Please do not disturb." Only two people could miss such a sign: a blind man or an inconsiderate church member. We were tired and wanted one quiet evening alone with our children. Our kids were ecstatic as we spread a plastic tablecloth on the floor of our living room, enjoyed a "pretend" picnic together, and began to watch some family-friendly entertainment on TV. Just then, the doorbell rang. It was like the ice witch ruling Narnia, all four of us sat like frozen creatures. The doorbell rang again. We continued to sit in stunned silence, but inwardly I seethed. Since no one in our church was blind, who would be so bull-headed and obnoxious to ignore our sign? The doorbell rang again. We just looked at each other, but no one made moved. Finally, the doorbell ringer gave up and left us alone. If my family had a "Daddy Gold Star" award, I think they would've pinned it on me. They knew even though I worked hard, I put them first and guarded time with them.

Retreats

Medical researchers identified a phenomenon labeled "Stress-induced Analgesia" (SIA). This is a reduced pain response to stress when your brain's descending pain-inhibitory circuits send a message to your body mediating your pain. Essentially, the brain provides numbness to your body as a protective measure in response to mental anxiety or trauma. When SIA wears off, long distance runners call it "hitting the wall." Your mental toughness may be reinforced by the amygdala (the emotion-processing center in your brain) to continue the race and fight through the wall. If so, noradrenaline floods your bloodstream and suppresses the transmitters indicating pain. As a result, you ignore the pain, get a second wind, and finish the race through the wonders of stress-induced analgesia.

Spaite (1) discussed the phenomenon of ministry-induced analgesia whereby clergy under stress may work themselves into a state of pain relief without realizing it. You work long hours. You rarely, if ever, take a day off or vacation. You want to "burn out, not rust out" and you work yourself into ministry-induced analgesia (MIA) followed by a crash.

I entered the Lakefront 50K in Chicago several years ago. None of my family went with me since it required an overnight stay and they would've been bored to tears while I attempted to complete an ultramarathon. I drove to Chicago after work on Friday. Family friends in the Windy City were gone for the weekend and graciously allowed me to stay at their home. I arrived about 10:00 P.M. or so and knew I needed a good night's sleep. Such was not the case. I was restless after the four-and-a-half-hour drive. I tried to watch TV, but I couldn't get the remote to work. I finally made my bed on the sofa and tried to sleep. I lay awake wondering if my alarm would wake me at the appointed hour. I was also concerned about getting to the location of the race on time. Needless to say, it was a fitful night of sleep.

On Saturday, I grabbed some breakfast and made my way to the race with about thirty minutes to spare. One critical mistake I made was buying a new pair of running shoes without breaking them in sufficiently. Shortly after starting, I knew they were too tight. Should I retreat and change my shoes or just "gut it out"? I decided on the latter. I finished the race with bloody toenails, but I was exhilarated since I accomplished my goal. I received my medal, my free food, and my new race shirt and headed for my car.

I thought I'd be exhausted, but I had a strange rush of

adrenaline. I departed Chicago thinking I might have to pull into a rest stop, but I never did. When I got home, I told my family about my triumph and then said, "I'm gonna lay down and get some well-deserved sleep." I threw myself on the bed, flipped on the TV and waited for my eyes to close. I couldn't sleep. I kept waiting for drowsy eyelids, my body to relax, and the sweet relief of sleep to come, but I was surprised. I had a surge of energy. Now, keep in mind, I drove four hours to Chicago after a full day of work, slept on a sofa, didn't sleep well and ran a 50K along the Chicago Lakefront with bloody toenails. I drove another four hours home and wasn't sleepy!

I decided to tackle one of the projects on my "Honey-Do List." I made my way up the stairs and started taking down the wallpaper in my daughter's room. My endorphins were releasing relentlessly. I was in project mode the rest of the weekend and into the first of the week. I was on a marathoner's high until Thursday! Then I collapsed. I had no energy. All I could do was sleep. In fact, my depressed condition lasted for about a week until I could get my physical and emotional equilibrium back in sync.

With "ministry-induced analgesia," you keep going. Your mind is telling your body: "You can make one more visit. You can take one more meeting. You can go to one more hospital room. You can do one more counseling session. You can handle one more crisis." You think you're invincible and then – *THUNK*! Your mind and body shut down and you have no energy. The diagnosis, my friend, is ministry-induced analgesia.

Once a pastor finally does go on vacation two days or more may pass before the endorphins dissipate and then overwhelming fatigue emerges. Vacations are vital for staying power. You must guard your vacation time for its restorative powers. Timely and lengthy vacations reconnect you with your family. According to a 2017 social media survey conducted by church consultant, Thom Rainer, nearly half of pastors take zero to two weeks of vacation a year.

Of the pastors who participated in my study, the two who neglected this practice were also the two struggling the most emotionally. As church growth expert, Peter Wagner, once stated, "If you are a good pastor, every year you need a vacation. If you are a bad pastor, every year your congregation needs a vacation from you."

Five years prior to our interview, Evan was approaching burnout. The president of the church council "took the bull by the horns" and granted him a sabbatical. He was given three months. He took "half of it one summer and half the next." The first summer he went to Cedar Lake Retreat in Wisconsin, part of the Pastor's Retreat Network. There are two additional sites in Texas and Ohio. The only requirement placed on him while at Cedar Lake was he and his wife had to share one meal a day with the other clergy and spouses. Otherwise, he was free to do what he wished whether he was reading or engaging in recreation or any other pursuits. The next summer, a member of his congregation offered him the use of a secluded lake home. The only request made of him by the owner was to mow the grass once a week. Both of these experiences were beneficial for Evan because he was able to restore his creative energies and motivated to return to his work with renewed zeal.

A change of pace is helpful for a minister to recuperate, receive inspiration, or gain perspective. Those involved in care-giving professions are under heavy mental and emotional demands. Taking advantage of this practice gives you a break and helps you escape everyday stresses and tension. Oswald (2) believed clergy need opportunities to de-role. They need spiritual nurture and adequate rest. It's worthy of note most of those utilizing this practice experienced some type of epiphany or gained some sort of strategy to help manage stress. At a five-day conference on prayer, Ben was exposed to principles he adopted as a regular practice. His zeal was so great, he purchased materials from the conference he reviewed repeatedly and they were a great source of strength and wisdom for him.

A series of both acute and chronic stressors grew nearly

unbearable for Chet and his wife. Though he was ready to resign, he and his wife reconsidered because of the encouragement they received from a renowned inspirational speaker. He returned to his church with renewed vigor. Donna learned techniques she could implement to manage stress and also adopted a new approach to her role as a pastor. When she attended a stress management retreat, she confessed it was good to hear other ministers were dealing with similar struggles. The experience proved beneficial because she decided to "quit internalizing everything as though it's your fault." She not only appropriated relaxation techniques, but also learned to say, "No," and decided to start delegating responsibilities to the membership.

Part of Hank's catharsis occurred when he attended a conference and identified with a seminar speaker. Hank burst into tears when the facilitator confessed to the same feelings and anxieties he suffered. He no longer viewed himself as a pariah. The conference provided a variety of materials instrumental in educating him about mediating stress and seeking the help he desperately needed.

Rae Jean Proeschold-Bell, an assistant professor of health research at Duke University, told the *New York Times*, clergy are people who "tend to be driven by a sense of duty to God to answer every call for help from anybody, and they are virtually called upon all the time, 24/7." In research she conducted about the necessity for ministers to get more rest, she revealed, "We had a pastor in our study group who hadn't taken a vacation in eighteen years." With this kind of pressure, it's little wonder clergy now suffer from obesity, hypertension and depression at higher rates than most Americans. The *Times* went on to reveal in the past decade, clergy's use of antidepressants has risen and their life expectancy has fallen. Does God really intend such for His called ones?

Sabbaticals have long been a part of university life for the purpose of rest, reflection, and revitalization (3). As early as 1979, Hansel (4) recommended pastors be given the opportunities for a sabbatical as a break from ministry longer than the standard vacation. A sabbatical generally occurs in or following a seventh year of service.

In 2005, Ellison Research in Phoenix, Arizona, released a study among a representative sample of 872 Protestant church ministers nationwide. In the study, they explored the job situations of ministers in the United States. What is intriguing is the research discovered the average minister has been the senior pastor of his or her current church for 7.7 years. Both Southern Baptists (87%) and Methodists (74%) don't believe a pastor stays at his/her church long enough. There is any number of reasons why a pastor stays less than eight years, but I think there's a subtle correlation.

The Ellison Research found common reasons for changing jobs: desire to serve in a different community/region of the country (27%), promoted to a higher position (20%), wanting to pastor a larger church (16%), being transferred by the denomination (15%), and planting a new church (15%). Eighteen percent had other reasons: family needs, job frustration, seeking a new challenge, conflict within the church, and just wanting a change. If nearly one of five clergy wishes to change because of this latter reason, is it reasonable to assume a simple break granted by the congregation could save both a pastor and a church? Think of the cost and upheaval incurred by both parties every 7.7 years. For the church, there's the necessity to find an interim, the emotion of saying farewell to a parsonage family, the election of a search team, the seemingly glacial pace of receiving resumes, vetting candidates and finding the right fit. Once a candidate is selected, a negative vote could submarine the whole process and force the church to start again. Then there's the expense of moving a new church family to the community. This is money and energy better spent on kingdom advancement rather than clergy replacement.

On the flip side, the pastor and family now have to pack—again. Ellison Research also discovered the typical minister has been the senior pastor at three different churches during his/her career. The result is another home has to be sold and yet another secured. Children say good-bye to friends and make new ones. If the spouse is employed outside the home, another job has to be secured in another locale. The move to a different community means changing schools, hair stylists, doctors, and dentists; and adopting new traditions at another church. Could this upheaval be blunted if a church could provide its pastor an extended leave, especially if either party is feeling restless?

Mike Turner, pastor of the Lexington Baptist Church in Lexington, South Carolina, offers the following three suggestions for pastors who want to begin sabbatical discussions within their church:

1) Call your trusted lay leaders together for a social gathering. Ask them to consider a sabbatical policy and leave it to them without saying another word. Live with their decision.

2) Bring in denominational leaders who've been on a sabbatical to help explain the leave of absence. Ultimately, the issue is trust between a pastor and the lay leaders.

3) Have a specific project you can present to the church leaders: respite for the pastor, a project to benefit the church, and helping the pastor acquire new skills.

Many church growth experts agree a pastor is just gaining the reins of leadership in the sixth, seventh and eight years. With the lay of the land in view, he/she is better suited to cast vision for long-term plans. Sadly, the sixth or seventh year is when a pastor can start to feel the "itch" to make a change if he/she is frustrated. It can be a tenuous time for both parties. The way it's handled can determine which mouse gets the cheese. Evan and his church leaders agreed on a sabbatical. It gave both a chance to step back. The congregation realized they had a great pastor. Evan's holistic tune-up led to increased creativity and efficiency in his ministry. The result was two-fold: a stronger church and an improved pastor.

Counselor

In a July 25, 2019, interview with *USA Today*, author and therapist Lori Gottlieb (5) made the following observation: "With our physical health, if there's some pain or something feels off in our bodies, we'll generally go to the doctor to get it checked out… But if something feels off emotionally… then usually what happens is we wait until we're having the emotional equivalent of a heart attack, and that's the time people land in therapy. And by then, you've suffered unnecessarily for a long time without needing to." Those in my study who utilized the help of a trained professional reaped or are reaping the rewards. Chet, Evan, Gwen, and Hank all sought counseling either for themselves, on behalf of their family, or for their marriage. Oftentimes, the demands of ministry are like trying to put suntan lotion on your back. You can't do it without some help.

Evan met a therapist through a pastor's gathering. The therapist invited a group of ministers to meet twice a month during the school year for three years at no charge. Evan took advantage of the opportunity. It held great value for him since he felt it was a safe place to vent to colleagues and all of them were able to address various issues in their lives. Each pastor took a turn discussing any issues and "that allowed me to take care of myself, to be emotionally involved with people." It just provided a safe place for him to vent and share with other pastors. He later sought guidance when he sensed a loss of momentum in his work and suffering from a lack of creativity. Evan's long tenure at his church lends credence to this coping method.

When asked how she coped with the incredible series of events life threw her way, Gwen conceded, "I've gone to a counselor." For her, it started when her son ran away from home. She visited a counselor "at least once a month." Later she humorously stated, "God has kept me out of any institution."

She characterized her sessions as a success. Gwen and her husband visited a counselor for assistance with "some marital stressors" during their time as co-pastors. The counselor diagnosed her husband as "living a life incongruent with who he was." Gwen's husband admitted he didn't want to be a pastor. To his credit, he stepped aside as co-pastor and Gwen assumed the senior pastorate. Apparently, such a positive result gave Gwen confidence to engage the services of a counselor after her son's rebellion. She continued her monthly visits.

Hank was "a little leery" of seeking help initially. He battled "extreme anxiety and depression." He was motivated to see a psychiatrist after two significant events. The first was attending a conference where a colleague emerging from an episode of severe stress recommended the value of professional help. Next came the night when "I found myself sitting in the dark" with a gun. For three hours he stared out the window "totally dumb and decided I was done." He admitted, "I started feeling stupid." He couldn't comprehend how everything at church and with his family could go so well and yet he was battling depression.

The counselor referred Hank to a psychiatrist for his medication. He was in counseling for two and a half months and the process helped "as far as how to deal with situations, how to deal with stress and things." Even though he was in therapy, he chose not to make it public. He traveled two and a half hours to see his counselor. In part, he worked through issues related to his "rough childhood." He also worked through his family history of depression, bipolar issues, and suicide. His opinion is "it's work" to get through difficult times and "you can't do it by yourself." As he began to talk about these areas, he understood not only the spiritual aspects but said "There can be an illness," even a "chemical issue."

The topic of stress in the pastorate was so personal and relevant to Hank he admitted his motivation and willingness to participate in this study. "That reason is such an issue to me right now" because he was suffering from "burnout." In his battle with extreme anxiety and depression, he was considering a thirty-day sabbatical. When I spoke with Hank in a follow-up discussion, the sessions as well as the medication were efficacious in moderating his stress.

McBurney (6) wrote, "Ministers are human beings, and the quicker they recognize their humanity, face their limitations, and get help when they need it, the sooner they begin to escape terrible consequences." Whether short or long-term, private or group, "nothing is shameful or weak about deciding to explore therapy as an option – in fact, it is a sign of strength and self-protection" (7). Therapy should be considered a safe place. Gross (8) asserted pastors suffering stress need the services of a professional counselor as part of a program to cope with "bottled-up feelings and the burnout dimension."

How you handle your stress is a decision only you can make. If you choose not to take any action, chances are you'll be one who exits the ministry prematurely with lower self-esteem, a poor quality of life, and jaded views of the church, the ministry, and even God. Your other option is to use the material in this book and put it into practice immediately. You can learn from the mistakes as well as successes of others. After all, the second mouse gets the cheese. With the proper coping strategies in place, you can cross glory's finish line with your head up, your sanity intact, and the sound of your heavenly Father saying, "Well done, good and faithful servant, enter into the joys prepared for you!"

CLERGY STRESS SELF ASSESSMENT

This *Clergy Stress Self Assessment* is designed to assist you in discovering whether you have enough stress coping strategies in place.

Score Sheet

To complete the score sheet, read the *Clergy Self-Assessment Questionnaire* and place a number based on the following four criteria in the box beside each question number.

Score Accuracy of this Statement

0   No

1   Seldom

2   Some of the time

3   Most or all of the time

1	2	3	4	5	6	7	8	9	10	11
12	13	14	15	16	17	18	19	20	21	22
23	24	25	26	27	28	29	30	31	32	33
34	35	36	37	38	39	40	41	42	43	44
45	46	47	48	49	50	51	52	53	54	55
56	57	58	59	60	61	62	63	64	65	66

Write the total of each <u>vertical</u> column in the boxes below.

CLERGY SELF ASSESSMENT

This tool should help you see more clearly areas where you are not properly engaged in alleviating your stress.

Questionnaire

1. I know I have a divine call to the ministry.

2. My family supports my call to the ministry.

3. I have a time of personal prayer/meditation every day.

4. I have a close friend of the same gender in my congregation.

5. I take a one-week vacation every year.

6. I have a time of personal Bible reading every day.

7. I read a newspaper at least once a week.

8. I go to a professional counselor for help with personal issues.

9. I exercise enough to break a sweat at least once a week.

10. I take a day off every week.

11. I take the time to disciple another person at least once a month.

12. If I feel like a failure, God's call on my life motivates me to persevere.

13. Members of my family never resent my profession.

14. My personal prayer time is a regular discipline I enjoy.

15. I have at least one close friend I spend time with who is not part of my congregation.

16. I attend at least one professional conference each year.

17. I do not count sermon preparation as part of my regular personal Bible reading.

18. I read a variety of periodicals.

19. I have no reservations about seeking the help of a professional therapist.

20. I like to go for a walk or just be active outdoors at least three times a week.

21. If I miss a day off one week, I will make up for it the next week.

22. I have invested in people in my congregation who make my job easier.

23. My calling is in line with my best gifts and the kind of work I enjoy.

24. My spouse enthusiastically supports my ministry.

25. My personal prayer time refreshes me.

26. I have a cluster of friends with whom I can just be myself.

27. I get away for a personal, professional or spiritual retreat at least once a year.

28. I read the Bible for personal enrichment at least five times a week.

29. I read fiction or non-fiction books that are not related to my profession.

30. I believe the services of a professional counselor are worth the time and money.

31. Strenuous exercise is part of my weekly routine.

32. I take a day off even if members of my congregation object.

33. I regularly teach spiritual leadership to key influencers in my congregation.

34. Memories of my divine call remind me I am in the proper career.

35. My family believes I put them first and my church always comes second.

36. My personal prayer time is separate from my ministry preparation prayer time.

37. There are people in my church who protect me if or when others in church attack me.

38. I take my full complement of vacation days each year.

39. I read more than three or four verses of Scripture a day for personal meditation.

40. Solving word puzzles or just reading a book is a pleasant diversion for me.

41. I have a trusted professional colleague to whom I can vent or seek advice.

42. I have a weekly hobby I enjoy which requires some degree of physical exertion.

43. I do not feel guilty when I take a day off every week.

44. I have trained people in my church who help reduce my ministry obligations.

45. I believe God's call on my life is irrevocable.

46. My best friend is a member of my family.

47. I am intentional about taking time every day to pray.

48. I have a group of friends I meet with regularly for accountability and affirmation.

49. I take my full allotment of professional development days each year.

50. I meditate on God's Word each day apart from my ministerial preparation.

51. Material I read from books is used for my teaching, preaching and leadership.

52. I have a mentor and follow the exhortation provided by such an individual.

53. I engage in physical activity which elevates my heart rate at least three times a week.

54. I will not interrupt my day off unless there is an extreme ministry emergency.

55. Our church is moving in the right direction because of leaders I have developed.

56. God affirms my call on a regular basis.

57. My family is a refuge for me from my ministry responsibilities.

58. I do not start a day without taking the time to pray.

59. I have at least one friend in my church I can call when I need any help.

60. I am absent from the church property at least three Sundays a year.

61. I believe I need devotional time in God's Word apart from sermon preparation.

62. I enjoy reading a wide variety of resources during the course of a week.

63. I visit or plan to visit a professional therapist for help.

64. My weekly discipline of physical activity is a high priority for me.

65. I guard my day off with a vengeance.

66. I have key leaders in my church who would "take a bullet" for me.

Clergy Stress Self-Assessment Analysis

To compute totals for this Assessment Analysis, transfer vertical columns' scores on the Score Sheet on page 213 to boxes A – K. For example, write the total of the scores in boxes 1, 12, 23, 34, 45, & 56 in box A below. Box B would include totals for 2, 13, 24, 35, 46, & 57, and so on until you complete the grid.

A	B	C	D	E	F	G	H	I	J	K

If you scored 0-6 in a column, place a "P" next to the coping strategy on the next page.

If you scored 7-12 in a column, place an "M" next to the coping strategy on the next page.

If you scored 13-18 in a column, place a "C" next to the coping strategy on the next page.

Coping Strategies

A._____ Divine Call   G. _____ Reading

B._____ Family Support   H. _____ Counselor

C. _____ Prayer   I. _____ Exercise

D. _____ Relationships   J. _____ Day Off

E. _____ Retreats   K. _____ Leadership

F. _____ Scripture   Development

Application of Coping Behavior

A score of 0-6 indicates you are *passively-engaged* and not seeking to moderate your stress through these behaviors.

A score of 7-12 indicates you are *moderately-engaged* and acknowledge the necessity to moderate your stress through these behaviors.

A score of 13-18 indicates you are *competently-engaged* and committed to alleviating your stress through these behaviors.

Individuals *passively-engaged* employ five or fewer coping behaviors.

Individuals *moderately-engaged* employ six to seven coping behaviors.

Individuals *competently-engaged* employ at least eight coping behaviors.

Clergy *passively-engaged* in five or fewer stress coping behaviors trend toward truncated pastorates and a lower quality of life.

Clergy *moderately-engaged* in six or seven stress coping behaviors are not as committed to the process and may be at risk in both career and quality of life.

Clergy *competently-engaged* in at least eight stress coping behaviors trend toward lengthy, stable pastorates and a higher quality of life.

WORKS CITED

CHAPTER 1

1. Greenleaf, R. K. (1977). *Servant leadership: A journey into the nature of legitimate power and greatness.* New York: Paulist Press, p. 228.

2. London, H. B., Jr., & Wiseman, N. B. (2003). *Pastors at greater risk: Real help for pastors from pastors who've been there.* Ventura, California: Regal Books.

3. Friedman, E. H. (1985). *Generation to generation: Family process in church and synagogue.* New York, NY: Guilford Press.

4. Hart, A. D. (2003). In London, H. B., Jr., & Wiseman, N. B. (2003). *Pastors at greater risk: Real help for pastors from pastors who've been there.* Ventura, California: Regal Books, 177.

5. Hall, T. (1997). The personal functioning of pastors: A review of empirical research with implications for pastors. *Journal of Psychology and Theology, 25,* 240-253.

6. Anderson, C. & Stark, C. (1988). Psychosocial problems of job relocation: Preventive roles in industry. *Social Work 33,* 38-41.

7. Quick, J. C., Nelson, D. L., & Quick, J. D. (1990). *Stress and challenge at the top: The paradox of the successful executive.* England: John Wiley & Sons Ltd., p. 22.

8. Frost, P. J. (2003). *Toxic emotions at work.* Boston, Massachusetts: Harvard Business School Press, pp. 32-33.

9. Marshall, J. & Cooper, C. L. (1979). *Executives under pressure: A psychological study.* New York, NY: Praeger Publishers, Praeger Special Studies.

10. Quick, Nelson & Quick (1990), op.cit., p. 54.

11. Ammons, P. Nelson, J., & Wodarski, J. (1982). Surviving corporate moves: Sources of stress and adaptation among corporate executive families. *Family Relations, 31,* 207-212.

12. Oswald, R. M. (1991). *Clergy Self-care: Finding a balance for effective ministry.* New York City: An Alban Institute Publication, pp. 26-27.

CHAPTER 2

1. Chun, D. (2006, November 18). Pastors often succumb to job burnout due to stress, low pay. "Island Life" in *The Honolulu Advertiser.* Retrieved September 28, 2007, from:

http://the.honoluluadvertiser.com/article/2006/Nov/18/il/
FP611180330.html .

2. Vroom, V. H. & Jago, A. G. (2007). The role of the situation in leadership. *American Psychologist, 62*(1), 17-24.

3. Iorg, J. (2011). *The case for Antioch: A biblical model for a transformational church.* Nashville, Tennessee: B& H Publishing Group.

4. McMinn, M. R., Lish, R. A., Trice, P. D., Root, A. M., Gilbert, N., & Yap, A. (2005). Care for pastors: Learning from clergy and their spouses. *Pastoral Psychology, 53*(6), 563-581.

5. Kotter, J. P. (1999) Leading change: The eight steps to transformation. In Conger, J. A., Spreitzer, G. M., Lawler III, E. E. (Eds.), (1999). *The leader's change handbook: An essential guide to setting direction and taking action.* (pp. 87-99) San Francisco: Jossey-Bass Publishers.

6. Wheaton, B. (1997). The nature of chronic stress. In B. H. Gottlieb (Ed.), *Coping with chronic stress* (pp. 43-73). New York: Plenum Press, p. 59.

7. Qubein, N. R. (2011). Controlling change. Retrieved March 10, 2011, from http://www.nidoqubein.com/articledisplay.cfm?aid=21 .

CHAPTER 3

1. Blume, B. (July 8, 2010), "Church control is top reason for forced pastor terminations in S.C." *The Baptist Courier*, p. 1.

2. Miller, K. A. (1988). *Secrets of staying power: Overcoming the discouragements of ministry.* Waco, Texas: Christianity Today, Inc., p. 72.

3. Ibid., p. 72.

4. Hersey, P. & Blanchard, K. H. (1982). *Management of organizational behavior: Utilizing human resources* (4th ed.). Englewood Cliffs, New Jersey: Prentice-Hall, Inc.

5. Schermerhorn, Jr. J. R. (2005). *Management,* (8th ed.). USA: John Wiley & Sons, Inc.

6. Hersey, P. & Blanchard, op. cit., p. 153.

7. Hersey, P. & Blanchard, op. cit., p. 153.

8. Walters, R. (2008). *Letters to pastors.* United States of America: Xulon Press.

9. Hersey, P. & Blanchard, op. cit., p. 153.

10. Hersey, P. & Blanchard, op. cit., pp. 153-154.

CHAPTER 4

1. Frost, P. J. (2003). *Toxic emotions at work.* Boston, Massachusetts: Harvard Business School Press, p. 14.

2. Gray, R. (January 3, 2013). *Pastoral termination: an epidemic? How a church deals with conflict or disagreement with its pastor is critical in the ongoing spirit and life of the congregation.* Retrieved January 15, 2013,from

   http://www.baptistcourier.com/8049.article.print

3. Hoge, D. R. & Wenger, J. E. (2005). *Pastors in transition: Why clergy leave local church ministry.* Grand Rapids, Michigan: William B. Eerdman's Publishing Company.

4. Gray, op. cit., 2013.

5. Sanders, J. O. (1986). *Spiritual leadership.* Chicago: The Moody Bible Institute, p. 35.

6. Gladwell, M. (2008). *Outliers: the story of success.* New York, NY: Little, Brown and Company, p. 166.

7. Will. G. (2013, August 1). A destitute city pillaged its people. *Spartanburg Herald-Journal,* p. A6.

8. Owen, M. (2014). *No hero: the evolution of a Navy SEAL.* New York, New York: Dutton.

9. Gray, op. cit., 2013.

10. McLaughlin, C. (2003). *Arts of diplomacy: Lewis and Clark's Indian collection.* Seattle: University of Washington Press.

11. Christianity Today (2013, May). *Church to former pastors: Sorry!* Gleanings: important developments in the church and the world, p. 12.

CHAPTER 5

1. Hepburn, C. G., Loughlin, C. A. & Barling, J. (1997). Coping with chronic work stress. In B. H. Gottlieb (Ed), *Coping with chronic stress* (pp. 343-366). New York: Plenum Press.

2. Siburt, C. and Wray, D. (2002). Minister self-care #1 presented at the Christian Education Conference, January, 2002. Retrieved September 6, 2007, from http://cconline.faithsite.com/content.asp?CID=39581.

3. Lee, C. & Iverson-Gilbert, J. (2003). Demand, support, and perception in family-related stress among protestant clergy. *Family Relations, 52*(3), 249-257.

4. Krause, N., Ellison, C. G., & Wulff, K. M. (1998). Church-based emotional support, negative interaction, and psychological well-being: Findings from a national

sample of Presbyterians. *Journal for the Scientific Study of Religion, 34*(4), 725-741.

5. Clinton, J. R. (1988). *The making of a leader: Recognizing the lessons and stages of leadership development.* Colorado Springs, Colorado: Navpress.

6. Berry, C. R. (2003). *When helping you is hurting me: Escaping the messiah trap.* New York, New York: The Crossroad Publishing Company.

7. Ware, B. (2012). *The top five regrets of the dying*: *A life transformed by the dearly departing.* United States of America: Hay House, Inc.

8. Chand, S. R. (2011). *Cracking your church's culture code: Seven keys to unleashing vision & inspiration.* San Francisco, California: Jossey-Bass.

9. Owen, M. (2014). *No hero: the evolution of a Navy SEAL.* New York, New York: Dutton.

CHAPTER 6

1. Tichy, N. M. & Bennis, W. G. (2007). *Judgment: How winning leaders make great calls.* New York, New York: Penguin Group.

2. Owen, M. (2014). *No hero: the evolution of a Navy SEAL.* USA: Dutton, 2014, p. 213.

3. Spaite, D. (1999). *Time bomb in the church: Defusing pastoral burnout.* Kansas City, Missouri: Beacon Hill Press.

CHAPTER 7

1. Minirth, F., Hawkins, D., Meier, P. D., Flournoy, R. (1986). *How to beat burnout.* Chicago, IL: The Moody Bible Institute of Chicago.
2. Dingfelder, S. (2006). Socially isolated and sick. In A. L. Sutton (Ed.), *Stress-related disorders sourcebook* (2nd ed.). Detroit, MI: Omnigraphics, Inc.
3. McMinn, Mr. R., Lish, R. A., Trice, P. D., Root, A. M., Gilbert, N., & Yap, A. (2005). Care for pastors: Learning from clergy and their spouses. *Pastoral Psychology, 53*(6), 563-581.
4. Roach, D. (2011). Survey: Pastors feel privileged and positive, though discouragement can come. Retrieved March 12, 2015, from http://www.lifeway.com/Article/Research-Survey-Pastors-feel-privileged-and-positive-though-discouragement-can-come
5. London, H. B., Jr., & Wiseman, N. B. (2003). *Pastors at greater risk: Real help for pastors from pastors who've been there.* Ventura, California: Regal Books.

6. Miller, K. A. (1988). *Secrets of staying power: Overcoming the discouragements of ministry.* Waco, Texas: Christianity Today, Inc.

7. Hall, T. (1997). The personal functioning of pastors: A review of empirical research with implications for pastors. *Journal of Psychology and Theology, 24,* 240-253.

8. Gladwell, M. (2008). *Outliers: The story of success.* New York, NY: Little, Brown, and Company.

CHAPTER 8

1. Wade, D. D. & Lunsford, J. D. (February 1989). *A guide for prescribed fire in southern forests.* Forest Service Southern Region: United States Department of Agriculture, Technical Publication R8-TP 11, p. 2.

2. Owen, M. (2014). *No hero: the evolution of a Navy SEAL.* USA: Dutton, 2014, p. 212.

3. Ibid., p. 213.

4. Hepburn, C. G., Loughlin, C. A. & Barling, J. (1997). Coping with chronic work stress. In B. H. Gottlieb (Ed.), *Coping with chronic stress* (pp. 343-366). New York: Plenum Press.

5. Tichy, N. M. & Bennis, W. G. (2007). *Judgment: How winning leaders make great calls.* New York, New York: Penguin Group, p. 51.

6. Ibid.

7. Greenleaf, R. K. (1977). *Servant leadership: A journey into the nature of legitimate power and greatness.* New York: Paulist Press, p. 226.

8. Lee, C. & Iverson-Gilbert, J. (2003). Demand, support, and perception in family-related stress among protestant clergy. *Family Relations, 52*(3), 249-257.

9. Quick, J. C., Quick, J. D., Nelson, D. L., & Hurrell, Jr., J. J. (1997). *Preventive stress management in organizations.* Washington, D.C.: American Psychological Association.

10. Op. cit., Tichy & Bennis, 2007.

CHAPTER 9

1. Mostofsky, E., Penner, E., & Mittleman, M. (March 4, 2014). Outbursts of anger as a trigger of acute cardiovascular events: A systematic review and meta-analysis. *European Heart Journal.*

2. Miller, K. A. (1988). *Secrets of staying power: Overcoming the discouragements of ministry.* Waco, Texas: Christianity Today, Inc.

3. Greenfield, G. (2005). *The wounded minister: Healing from and preventing personal attacks.* Grand Rapids, MI: Baker Books, p. 201.

4. Leatz, C. A. & Stolar, M. W. (1993). *Career success/personal stress: How to stay healthy in a high-stress environment.* United States of America: McGraw-Hill, Inc.

5. Schneider, S. & Kastenbaum, R. (1993). Patterns and meanings of prayer in hospice caregivers: An exploratory study. *Death Studies (17)*6, 471-485), p. 476.

6. Hulme, W. E., (1985). *Managing stress in ministry.* San Francisco: Harper & Row, Publishers, p. 59.

7. Leatz & Stolar, op. cit.

8. Hulme, op. cit., p. 72.

9. Foster, R. J. (1978). *Celebration of discipline: The path to spiritual growth.* San Francisco: Harper Collins, p. 69.

10. Bridges, J. (2003). Pursuing and practicing personal holiness. In H. B. London, Jr., & N. B. Wiseman, (Eds.). *Pastors at greater risk: Real help for pastors from pastors who've been there,* p. 276.

11. Mickey, P. A. & Ashmore, G. W. (1991). *Clergy families: Is normal life possible?* Grand Rapids, Michigan: Zondervan Publishing House, p. 115.

12. Leatz & Stolar, op. cit., p. 183.

13. Thames, B. J. & Thomason, D. J., (2002). Stress management-taking charge. *National Ag Safety Database.* 04/2002. Retrieved December 5, 2008, from http://www.cdc.gov/nasd/docs/d001201-d001300/d001246/d001246.html.

14. Metzger, C. (2003). Self/inner development of educational administrators: A national study of urban school district superintendents and college deans. *Urban Education (38)*6, 665-687.

15. Chun, D. (2006, November 18). Pastors often succumb to job burnout due to stress, low pay. "Island Life" in *The Honolulu Advertiser.* Retrieved September 28, 2007, from http://the.honoluluadvertiser.com/article/2006/Nov/18/il/FP611180330.html .

16. Mickey & Ashmore, op. cit., p. 115.

CHAPTER 10

1. Spaite, D. (1999). *Time bomb in the church: Defusing pastoral burnout.* Kansas City, Missouri: Beacon Hill Press.

2. Oswald, R. M. (1991). *Clergy self-care: Finding a balance for effective ministry.* New York City: An Alban Institute Publication.

3. Quick, J. C., Quick, J. D., Nelson, D. L., & Hurrell, Jr., J. J. (1997). *Preventive stress management in organizations.* Washington, D. C.: American Psychological Association.

4. Hansel, T. (1979). *When I relax I feel guilty.* Elgin, IL: David C. Cook.

5. VanDenburgh, B. (2019). Writer dispels myths about therapy. *USA Today*, July 25, 2019, p. 3D.

6. McBurney, L. (1985). In Merrill, D., *Clergy couples in crisis: The impact of stress on pastoral marriages.* Waco, Texas: Word Books, p. 67.

7. Leatz, C. A. & Stolar, M. W. (1993). *Career success/personal stress: How to stay healthy in a high-stress environment.* United States of America: McGraw-Hill, Inc., p. 198.

8. Gross, P. R. (1989). Stress and burnout in ministry: A multivariate approach. *Lutheran Theological Journal, 23,* 27-31.

Made in United States
Orlando, FL
19 January 2024